On the Move

BOOKS BY
The Columbia Partnership Ministry Partners

George W. Bullard Jr.
Every Congregation Needs a Little Conflict
Pursuing the Full Kingdom Potential of Your Congregation

Richard L. Hamm
Recreating the Church:
Leadership for the Postmodern Age

Edward H. Hammett
Reaching People under 40 while Keeping People over 60:
Being Church to All Generations

Spiritual Leadership in a Secular Age:
Building Bridges Instead of Barriers

Making Shifts without Making Waves:
A Coach Approach to Soulful Leadership

A full listing and description of TCP resources are available at
www.chalicepress.com and
www.thecolumbiapartnership.org

On the Move

Adding Strength, Speed, and Balance to Your Congregation

C. JEFF WOODS

CHALICE
PRESS

ST. LOUIS, MISSOURI

Cover image: Phil Ashley/Lifesize/GettyImages
Cover and interior design: Elizabeth Wright

Visit Chalice Press on the World Wide Web at
www.chalicepress.com

10 9 8 7 6 5 4 3 2 1   09   10   11   12   13   14

EPUB=978-08272-37378 • EPDF=978-08272-37385

Library of Congress Cataloging-in-Publication Data

Woods, Charles Jeffrey, 1958-
  On the move : adding strength, speed, and balance to your congregation / Jeff C. Woods.
      p. cm. – (TCP leadership series)
    ISBN 978-0-8272-2728-6
  1. Christian leadership. 2. Pastoral theology. 3. Church. I. Title.
  BV652.1.I43 2009
  254'.5–dc22

2009024544

Printed in the United States of America

Dedicated to...
Kandy, Brandon, and Kelsey
and all of the organizations
they will encounter.

Contents

Editor's Foreword

Inspiration and Wisdom for Twenty-First–Century Christian Leaders

You have chosen wisely in deciding to study and learn from a book published in **The Columbia Partnership Leadership Series** with Chalice Press. We publish for

- Congregational leaders who desire to serve with greater faithfulness, effectiveness, and innovation.
- Christian ministers who seek to pursue and sustain excellence in ministry service.
- Members of congregations who desire to reach their full kingdom potential.
- Christian leaders who desire to use a coach approach in their ministry.
- Denominational and parachurch leaders who want to come alongside affiliated congregations in a servant leadership role.
- Consultants and coaches who desire to increase their learning concerning the congregations and Christian leaders they serve.

The Columbia Partnership Leadership Series is an inspiration- and wisdom-sharing vehicle of The Columbia Partnership, a community of Christian leaders who are seeking to transform the capacity of the North American church to pursue and sustain vital Christ-centered ministry. You can connect with us at www.TheColumbiaPartnership.org.

Primarily serving congregations, denominations, educational institutions, leadership development programs, and parachurch organizations, the Partnership also seeks to connect with individuals, businesses, and other organizations seeking a Christ-centered spiritual focus.

We welcome your comments on these books, and we welcome your suggestions for new subject areas and authors we ought to consider.

George W. Bullard Jr., Senior Editor
GBullard@TheColumbiaPartnership.org

The Columbia Partnership,
332 Valley Springs Road, Columbia, SC 29223-6934
Voice: 803.622.0923, www.TheColumbiaPartnership.org

Introduction

The Importance of Agility

Picture the most agile animal you have ever witnessed in the wild. Recall its ability to maneuver around obstacles, avoid threats, and focus upon its destination. Recollect the amazing display of strength and speed with each movement made under complete control. Imagine your organization performing like that. This book will help your organization become more agile by enhancing strength, speed, and balance.

Agility matters. Only organizations that prepare well and perform competently will be able to adapt to the environmental changes that the future will bring. Many have claimed that only the fast will survive. But today's organizations need more than just speed. They need agility. Some organizations have become so lean that they have sacrificed health. Others respond to the latest fad or guru gimmick to the point where they operate in an "out of control" manner, devoid of any strategy. Other organizations concentrate too heavily on one aspect to the neglect of all other members, departments, and tasks. This book will show you how to develop your organization into a faster, more responsive one while at the same time expanding the breadth of your organizational strengths. Agility is strength and speed under control. The best athletes are those who can display both speed and focus while engaging in the required task. Read on to learn how to develop your organization so that it can respond with both speed and flexibility when needed.

Three Assumptions

An organization needs three qualities to be agile. First, it must be alive. It is difficult to be agile if you are dead. Yet organizations try to respond to twenty-first–century problems with twentieth-century solutions. They focus on cosmetic details when their vital signs are sending off warning signals. They mount a dead horse at high noon. Other organizations are like hot air balloons. They cast off whatever is within reach in order to rise higher and higher for the moment, only to discover upon landing that they lack the necessary provisions to survive until the next flight. Organizations must feed their vital signs in order to stay alive.

Second, in order to be agile, an organization must have multiple leaders focused on multiple outcomes. I admire all of the attention that "vision" has received in organizations over the last decade or two, but too often organizations have confused "singularly focused" with "singularly skilled." Agile organizations are not myopic. They must be clear about where they are headed, but they must simultaneously develop the organization for the next major opportunity or the next major shift in culture. Such diversity of outcomes requires a diversity of leaders. An organization may have a CEO or a chairperson or a president or a pastor as its most visible leader, but everyone in those roles must recognize the need to involve others in leadership tasks and responsibilities. Agile organizations develop leaders in every facet of organizational life.

Third, agile organizations need balance. Teeter too much in either direction on a number of continuums and the organization will drag weight to one side or the other. Focus too much on the supply side and the organization will lose touch with its constituents. Focus too much on the demand side and the organization will promise beyond its delivery capabilities. Focus too much on accountability and see what happens to the mood of the staff. Focus too much on empowerment, and some will not perform. Lopsided organizations are not agile. Agile organizations are balanced organizations.

In a moment, I will explore these three assumptions in a bit more detail, but first a few thoughts about the intended audience.

Who Should Read This Book

Anyone who cares about improving organizations will benefit from reading this book. Chances are that you picked up this book with one particular organization in mind, such as your church or workplace, but this book will encourage you to think about the range of organizations to which you belong in order transfer the strength discoveries from one to the needs of another. One of the breakthroughs about leadership skills in the last several years is that leadership skills are transferable.[1] The same is true of organizational strengths. Learn how to develop a vision in one organization and it will be easier to do the same in another one. Good process is good process no matter where it takes place. Likewise, tools that develop people will work in any setting.

This book will offer both a comprehensive view of organizations as well as specific help in key areas, but it is not a quick fix. If quick fixes worked, this book would be much shorter. But they don't. This book will help you strengthen your organization. It will help you become more responsive to a variety of opportunities and, most importantly, it will show you how to develop a more balanced organization. Developing multiple equilibrium points throughout your organization requires time, energy, and knowledge. Balances and quick fixes don't mix.

This book is practical in nature. I am a practical theorist. I will provide some theoretical background in the introduction because I believe that all models need a sound conceptual base, but each subsequent chapter will provide detailed help in how to surface a vision, launch a fundraising campaign, deal with conflict, and even transform. Following the introduction, this book can be read from the inside out rather than in a linear fashion. For instance, if organizational transformation interests you most, turn to the section on change and begin reading about how to develop a passion for change as well as how to help the organization mature. If working directly with people most interests you, turn to section 3 and begin reading about potential and performance issues. If you picked up a copy in order to promote purpose and focus, turn to section 2 to read about mission and results. I encourage you to begin reading where your passion lies. Skim the sections to discover the range of what is contained in the book, but go ahead and read according to where your curiosity falls. My only caution in reading and implementing a single chapter is that you should not view any single chapter as a quick fix for your entire organization. Remember, agile organizations are strong, fast, *and* balanced.

This book is about organizations rather than individuals. This text is about organizational development rather than leadership development. Instead of focusing upon the specific skills that you alone need as the leader of your organization, the book will help you add strength, speed, and balance to your organization so that the organization can better serve its staff and its constituents.

You may want to read this book with a team. The questions at the end of each chapter lend themselves well to group study or classroom discussion. It may also be fun to compare your answers to the surveys at the end of each chapter. The assessment pieces will probably confirm some areas where strength and speed already exist as well as provide the needed urgency to make changes in other arenas. I believe that this book will help leaders at every level gain a better understanding of their strengths and weaknesses, preferences and personalities. Marcus Buckingham argued that only twenty percent of employees working in large organizations report being in a position where they do what they do best everyday.[2] This book helps leaders and members to position themselves where they should be in the organization. If you picked up a copy of this book with the intention of personally transforming your organization into an agile one, you may want to think about involving a small group of like-minded individuals in order to develop an action plan. New ideas and new visions can be read and developed by individuals, but are implemented best in teams.

Can the book really apply to all types of organizations? Yes. While the majority of the examples and illustrations will be drawn from religious organizations and nonprofits, the principles that strengthen organizations are transferable from one type of organization to another. Because I developed the model from a broad conceptual understanding of organizations, readers from every corner of organizational interest will be able to apply the principles to their churches, agencies, boards, schools, federations, or businesses.

As you read through the book, I encourage you to become an observer of organizations. You will be amazed at how much of an understanding you can acquire about a particular organization just by gaining a glimpse of it from one of its members. Consider how many organizations you have intersected with today. Did you drop your kids off at school this morning? What did you observe at the school? Did you drive to a workplace? How did you feel as you arrived? What histories and traditions in your workplace made you feel that way? Did you stop by a small business or recreation center after work? How were you treated as a customer? If you work from home, how many people did you network with today? What differences did you perceive within your network? You will gain more from the book if you are concurrently seeking to assess an organization based upon some of the criteria named in these pages, or are seeking to apply some of the principles contained within them.

Breadth and Depth

This book reveals how to strengthen your organization in both breadth and depth. From a breadth perspective, it identifies a full range of outcomes that leaders should be focusing upon in order to ensure both short-term triumphs and long-term vigor. It shows how to fortify your mission, vision, plans, communications, assets, decision-making processes, and more. The book will challenge you to think more deeply about your organization.

From a depth perspective, the book offers three layers of analysis in developing organizations. The first layer deals with elements present in every organization, namely: culture, purpose, people, assets, and change. By applying two different types of processes to each of these first-layer elements, the second layer then reveals twelve outcomes for organizational development. The book is organized around this middle layer: the layer of outcomes. Finally, the third layer shows the unique tensions that must be balanced in order to produce those outcomes on a long-term basis. Once again, the three layers are:

Layer One = Elements Common to Every Organization
Layer Two = Organizational Outcomes
Layer Three = Tensions and Balance

Background of the Agility Model

In this section, I briefly describe how each of the three layers was developed. If you are simply too anxious to read about the outcomes of the model rather than the background of the model, skip to the first section and return here only if your curiosity demands it.

In Search of a Framework

After leading hundreds of workshops on specific aspects of organizational life, about four years ago I began developing a more comprehensive approach to the subject. The drive to develop such a model surfaced from my inability to adequately respond to questions such as these: "How do you know that you are covering what you need to cover as a leader?" "What does the complete list of tasks look like?" "Who should be involved in leadership?" "Where does management end and leadership begin?" Those are fair questions. In response, I began to make lists that I would inevitably tear up after only a few weeks. I realized that a mere list would not suffice. I needed a framework. I needed a foundation for thinking about organizations in the twenty-first century. I began by reducing the content of organizations down to a common set of elements contained in every organization. After a few adjustments, I settled on the following elements: culture, purpose, people, assets, and change. Go ahead and try these elements out on your organization. I believe that you will find that each element is lodged somewhere in your church, team, board, school, or business. With this first layer of analysis complete, I began searching for a tool to apply to these elements that would produce a set of outcomes for all organizations to embrace. I have always believed that a fully developed organization has the best chance of responding to a rapidly changing world. I applied several potential typologies to my first layer of elements, including personality theories, mathematics, a simple "Do's, Don'ts, and Differences" typology, and left-sided and right-sided brain differences. I used cubes, spheres, circles, and ovals for frameworks. People who sat next to me on airplanes during this time must have thought I was crazy, as I drew elaborate sketches only to tear them up and start over. Over time, the metaphor of the brain began to surface as a helpful image. I discovered some pioneering work being done on the brain that became an adaptable framework for this model. The most readable description of the research that I found is contained in a book by Jeffrey Hawkins, entitled *On Intelligence*.[3]

Brain Theory

The foundations contained in some recent theories about how the brain functions formed the framework for which I had been searching. As I continued my analysis of organizations from layer one to layer two, I developed a way for leaders to process the sources of organizational input just as the brain does for the human body's sources of input. The more I researched the brain, the more the recent theories of how the brain actually functions fit my thinking regarding organizational development. The brain proved to be more than adequate in describing how to process elements of organizational life. Applying one set of brain activities to the sources of raw material contained in layer one yielded the precise set of organizational outcomes that I had been trying to define. Applying a second set of brain activities to these outcomes yielded a third layer of organizational activity, a layer of built-in organizational tensions that must be balanced in order to maintain organizational agility. Allow me to explain further.

For organizations, the sources of raw material contained in the first layer of organizational thinking—namely, culture, purpose, people, assets, and change—are analogous to the sources of input for the human body: eyes, ears, noses, touches, and tongues. Within a few seconds, the brain may process hundreds, even thousands of inputs from these sources with amazing accuracy. The brain is the ultimate model of strength and speed. Apply this concept to organizations: leaders are also called upon to make decisions based upon all of their sources of input, often as rapidly as possible due to the environment in which we now live. For instance, consider the task of calling or hiring a new staff member. In selecting a new member of the staff team, input about the organization's assets, complementary employee skills and performance, organizational norms and behaviors—all enter into the decision. Sources of input for organizations are inextricably linked, just as the sources of input are for the human brain. The brain detects that the eye is seeing a human face rather than a portrait on the wall by linking the semblance of a face with the presence of voice and smell and even touch. If a leader can learn to draw from these sources of input in a comprehensive, synergistic, and speedy manner, that leader is on the way toward developing an agile organization.

What makes this model work is the discovery that the brain is not as complex as previously thought. Previous attempts to build artificial intelligence all sought to develop the hearing process differently from the sight process, differently from the olfactory process, and so forth. But, one of the most recent and amazing discoveries in neuroscience is that the brain processes information from each of its senses in the same manner.[4] The brain does not have a special way of decoding hearing, and another way of decoding sight; it processes sight and sound the same way and uses the interactions of what is being sensed to make predictions about what will follow. In this agility model, I am suggesting that leaders process the organizational inputs from culture, concepts, people, assets, and changes in the same manner that our brains process input from our eyes, ears, noses, tongues, and touches. In this way, leaders can finally become the "brains of the outfit"—but I wouldn't share that analogy with anyone else too soon!

In the next section, I detail the first type of brain activity that I applied to layer one in order to produce the set of organizational outcomes contained in layer two, the layer that forms the outline of this book. In the subsequent section, I will detail a second brain activity that I used to produce the third layer of organizational development, the layer known as tensions.

Strength and Speed, Prediction and Testing, Incubation and Journey

As the brain receives various sources of input, it makes little predictions about what the body will encounter next. The brain strengthens its case for an accurate prediction by aggregating the sources of input received. The brain then works as quickly as possible in order to respond as quickly as possible. The brain delivers both strength and speed. If you are typing on a keyboard, your brain predicts the next command. If you are listening to a song, your brain predicts the next note. It even predicts the tone and the tempo from the strength of its data. If you are jogging along a trail, your brain predicts the next turn, the next sound you might hear, the next threat or opportunity you might encounter. Your brain strengthens your ability to respond to danger with the most appropriate reaction in the smallest amount of time possible. Your brain tests out those predictions to see if they come true and then adjusts accordingly. As your brain encounters similar situations it develops more speed of response. How long did it take you to learn your ABCs? How fast can you say them now? The ten outcomes in this book were developed using a similar process of "prediction" and "testing" for leaders. In order to strengthen the accuracy of its prediction and make more quality decisions, the brain draws from a variety of inputs. Upon evaluating those decisions, over time the brain also develops the ability to make quality decisions with ever-increasing speed. The brain is our source of strength and speed.

I use a number of metaphors to describe this model. One set of metaphors that has been helpful to some is the language of incubation and journey. Some view the "prediction" phase of leadership as *incubation* and the "testing" phase of leadership as *journey*. Thus, each source of input for the leader has both an incubation phase and a journey phase. Have you ever felt like you needed more "think time" as a leader? Ever felt like you were simply jumping from one task to the next without any time to breathe in between? If so, then you were experiencing all "journey" and no "incubation" as a leader. Leaders need time to process and ponder in order to produce. Each source of input (culture, purpose, people, assets, and change) needs some incubation time.

On the other hand, have you ever felt as if your organization was too wrapped up in process? Have you ever manufactured forty pounds of newsprint only to let it take up space on the shelf or in your assistant's computer? Ever develop a mission statement never to be read again? Leaders cannot incubate forever. At some point they must also take the organization for a ride. They must lead the journey. They must act. Action aimed at making a difference, not just making sure that everyone has been included, must also be part of a leader's repertoire of skills. Leaders must engage people in action, not just develop them for the journey.

Even though I believe that individuals are naturally gifted at either the incubation side or the journey side of leadership, both are needed in order to develop the organization. Leaders must balance strength and speed, prediction and testing, incubation and journey in order to produce a comprehensive set of outcomes.

Balancing Organizational Outcomes
Strength --Speed
Prediction---Testing
Incubation--Journey

Back to the Brain

The speed and strength activities of the brain describe one pair of brain functions. As the brain sends information up the layers of its neocortex, it is strengthening its case for an accurate prediction. As the brain evaluates these choices over time by sending information back down through these same layers of neocortex, it develops an ability to make quality decisions in less and less time. This first pair of "strength and speed activities," more accurately known as prediction and testing, help describe what an organization *does*. But, another pair of brain activities help us understand *how* the brain accomplishes these tasks.

With every task of leadership, an inherent tension is built in. In order to explain that tension, we will again turn toward the brain as a metaphor. Earlier, we learned that the brain processes input from all of its sources in the same way, regardless of whether that input is coming from the eyes, the ears, the nose, etc. The brain sends information both up and down in order to gain both strength and speed. But in what form does the information come into the brain? The brain receives information in two primary patterns or styles. The first type of information that the brain receives comes in the form of "coincident" patterns. For example, even though a face may slightly alter its expression as its lips move or it expresses emotion, another person will still recognize it as a face, indeed the same face that is speaking, through the brain's formation of a coincident pattern.[5] Without the formation of a coincident pattern, our brain might tell us that a different person is speaking every time an individual raises or lowers her voice or shifts her head from one side to the other. Without coincident patterns, you could never recognize one of your friends in all seasons, shapes, colors, moods, and modalities.

On the other hand, how does the brain recognize a song that the other face may be singing? That can only be done through the formation of a temporal pattern, one that changes over time.[6] The brain can only recognize a song over time, never all at once. Thus, the brain forms both coincident and temporal patterns in order to make sense of the world. The brain uses a coincident pattern to determine that the same individual is still singing even though the person is constantly changing facial expressions, and it uses a temporal pattern to enjoy the song.

In a similar manner, leaders of agile organizations make sense of both types of patterns that emerge from the inputs of culture, concepts, people, assets, and change in order to produce the outcomes desired by the various constituents of the organizations. Leaders use a coincident pattern to ensure progress on goals, but they must switch to a temporal pattern to discern whether or not those goals are having the desired impact over time. Coincident patterns enable accountability of performance, but it is the temporal pattern that provides the necessary empowerment that must also accompany the performance outcome. The tension between coincident and temporal patterns serves as the basis of the natural tensions built into each outcome of leadership. Unlike the dichotomy of incubation and journey, however, the concepts behind the dichotomy of coincident and temporal patterns adjust as we move from each source of input to the next. This will become evident as you read about the tensions associated with each outcome.

Theological Basis for the Model

Because I work in a religious context, I never present a new organizational concept without also providing a theological basis for it. The theological background for the concept of incubation and journey comes from Mark 4:26–29. The first part of this passage describes the parable of the seed. In this parable, Jesus describes two kinds of activity. One type of activity involves preparation. It is during the preparatory phase that the plant gains enough strength to burst through the soil. If our desire is for congregations to grow and develop, we must plant seeds of potential growth. We do this by sharing our faith with our friends, training leaders, asking people to give, and suggesting behavioral norms. This is incubation work. It is work that strengthens the members, the congregation, the judicatory, and the denomination. This phase of the work is less visible, but no less viable. It is impossible to observe the seed gaining strength. Leaders sometimes get anxious for visible signs of productivity from their labors. But, a farmer can do nothing to speed the growth of the seed. The farmer must trust that visible signs of growth will eventually ensue.

When the seed bursts through the soil, however, a new type of activity must now be embraced. The farmer must now feed, water, and care for the seed, protecting it from the harmful elements and nourishing its growth. These are journey activities. Once trained, others within the congregation or denomination must be continually challenged and supported in order to continue to grow and develop. Some leaders are better at "below the line" activities. They are better at incubation work. They take people to lunch, plant ideas, and point out the potential that others may not see in themselves. Other leaders are naturally adept at leading the journey. They long for action. They develop new programs, respond to opportunities, and spend resources in ways that make a difference. Agile congregations need both incubation and journey. They need both strength and speed. Agility requires both preparation as well as performance.

I will now describe each outcome in more detail. The outcomes presented below are balanced in terms of strength and speed. Half of the outcomes help to strengthen the organization while the other half enhance its speed. Each outcome also comes with a built-in tension that, if balanced, can also enhance the organization's agility.

The Agility Model Described in More Detail

Layer One–Elements Common to Every Organization
Layer Two–Organizational Outcomes
Layer Three–Tensions

A View from 10,000, 5,000, and 500 Feet

Have you ever been skydiving? I have, in my earlier, crazier, softer-headed days. The experience took place in college, during my freshman year when I had pledged a fraternity. Those who have taken similar actions will know that "pledging" requires the completion of several "tasks" in order to be accepted as a full, active member of the fraternity house. As I neared the end of the pledging process, my buddy, Greg, and I had completed nearly every requirement except one. We needed twelve on-campus activity hours and we had a total of zero heading into the final week of pledging. Even while we had poured our hearts and souls into this new fraternity adventure, we also were supposed to have joined a club on campus. We found ourselves faced with needing credit for twelve weekly meetings with only one week to go, a poorly planned calculation for an engineer and a statistician. Greg came up with the solution. If we joined the parachuting club, we could get all twelve hours in one weekend. Train on Friday; jump on Saturday. We signed up. We logged four contact hours in on Friday, but the Saturday wind jeopardized the remainder of our plan. After much discussion, the pilot agreed to take us up and drop the streamer. The pilot releases a streamer to see how far from the target the streamer lands, then the pilot makes a second pass and drops the parachuters a similar distance ahead of (or behind) the target. The streamer landed within an acceptable distance from the target to make the second pass. We were dropped from the plane. Then the wind gusted once again.

Since this was our first jump, we were ignorant of the problems ahead and just enjoyed the view. At 10,000 feet, one can see for miles. At this level, one does not really see buildings, but rather sections and areas of the city. The 10,000 feet view did not last long. At 5,000 feet, we could make out much more detail, but still had difficultly pinpointing particular locations or trouble spots. At 5,000 feet we also both began to realize, however, that the target was nowhere in sight. As we neared the ground, our goal shifted from hitting the target to avoiding danger. At 500 feet, power lines came into full view; woods became visible; and houses, rather than an airstrip, were all that we could see. Miraculously, we landed unharmed, except for our egos. Our four hours of training paid off as we each successfully navigated the last few sources of danger, with Greg landing beyond the woods and I just in front of them next to a set of power lines in the midst of someone's backyard. Even though we were both about four miles from our target, the 500–foot view provided enough motivation to put the newly acquired agility tools into play. We had avoided disaster. Thinking back, perhaps the experience was even more traumatic than we had originally thought, for Greg became a physician and I became a minister.

This book offers three distinct views of your organization. The first view is from 10,000 feet. A view from this level can only see the surface of the elements common to every organization. As you scan the sections of this book, you will be invited to ponder the culture, the purpose, the people, and the assets of your organization, but with no more instruction than that, it will be difficult to gain a very detailed view of the strengths and shortcomings of your organization. The 5,000 feet view changes everything. At this level, you will be able to begin assessing the relative strengths and weaknesses of your organization. You will learn about the types of outcomes that your organization should be producing and will be able to identify places to celebrate and as well as places that need more attention. But, it is only at the 500–foot level that the real dangers come into view. This is the level of tension within organizational life. This is the level where balance is absolutely critical to agility.

Layer One–the Raw Material of Organizations

While each organization is as unique as every other living organism, organizations do have some aspects in common. Every organization possesses certain kinds of *raw material*. The outcomes in this agility model were developed through an analysis of the *raw material* of organizations, elements common to all types of organizations. These elements are: culture, purpose, people, assets, and change. Every organization has *people*. The people of an organization have a collective *purpose*. In order for an organization to achieve anything with its purpose, it must have resources or *assets*. Dealing with assets presents choices, and choices always lead to *conflict*. Some conflicts are a natural result of personality differences, while other conflicts are signs of a need to *change*. The ways that an organization does all of these things will be influenced by its *culture*.

Layer Two–Multiple Outcomes and Multiple Leaders

This book is about organizational development. For that reason, the book is organized around the middle, or *outcomes*, layer. This book will help you and your leadership team better understand how to strengthen your organization according to ten defined outcomes. Each chapter focuses upon a particular product, absolutely achievable in your organization. Just as individuals focus on multiple outcomes, so do organizations. Consider all of the outcomes that you desire for yourself on any given day. You arose with a purpose in mind. But, before you could focus upon that purpose, you probably wanted to arrive at your destination in one piece. Once at your location, you desired to be productive, to make a difference in your corner of the world. You also desire to enjoy yourself, to better yourself, to care for someone else, to learn something, to be a positive influence on someone else, and to be a role model for those around you. Do we achieve each of these desired outcomes everyday? Probably not. But we *are* focused on multiple outcomes simultaneously everyday.

The heart of this agility model is its middle layer, which focuses upon organizational outcomes. Subsequent chapters will be organized around these outcomes. The multiple outcomes that I suggest for organizations are shown below.

Identity	Vision
Mission	Results
Potential	Performance
Capacity	Allocations
Passion	Maturity

Outcomes Derived from the Input of Culture

Every organization has an *iden-tity*. It has a past, a set of talents, and a set of turmoils. Discovering its identity greatly strengthens the organization. An organization's identity is uncovered through an analysis of its culture. Taking that identity on the road results in *vision*. As the organization lives out its identity, the members and constituents begin to see first hand the vision of what the organization can become.

CULTURE → Identity
CULTURE → Vision

Outcomes Derived from the Input of Purpose

Dealing with the incubation phase leads to the definition of an organization's *mission*. Businesses must decide what business they are in. Nonprofits must decide what mission they are in. Both must prioritize their narrowly defined missions from a full range of potential activities capable of consuming the organizations. Living out the mission leads to *results*. Agile leaders help an organization prioritize its concepts and ideas. Every organization must then prove to its constituents, through the demonstration of the speed of its results, that those concepts were indeed the right ones to embrace.

PURPOSE → Mission
PURPOSE → Results

Outcomes Derived from the Input of People

Incubating people in an organization leads to their development. Developing people increases the *potential* of the organization and greatly enhances its strength. While no source of input can be ignored, an organization will be no greater than the source of its potential as defined by the skills and attitudes of its members or employees. But developing people is only one-half of this equation. Increased potential may lead to increased performance, but not always. They require two separate skills sets and usually the attention of two separate leaders. Enhancing the potential of the organization involves meeting the needs of people, beginning with the most fundamental skills known to lead to productivity within the organization and moving up the scale until each individual is actualized in the organization.

PEOPLE → Potential
PEOPLE → Performance

Enhancing the *performance* of the organization involves discovering ways to encourage, empower, motivate, and inspire the members and employees of the organization to function at their highest level. Potential enhances strength and performance enhances speed.

Outcomes Derived from the Input of Assets

Incubating the assets of an organization leads to *capacity*, enhancing an additional dimension of strength. An organization that has developed every leader to his or her fullest potential and inspired each to 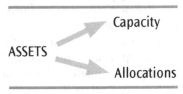 perform skillfully can still be constrained by a lack of resources. Most businesses view this aspect of leadership as the bottom line. But even leaders of nonprofit organizations must garner assets in order to survive. Taking those assets on a journey involves allocating them to appropriate causes. Raising resources and allocating those resources are two essential outcomes.

Outcomes Derived from the Input of Change

The only way that an individual will change is if he or she desires to do so. The same is true of organizations. Agile leaders unmask the *passion* within an organization and then chan- 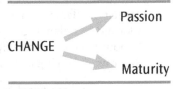 nel that passion toward mature and desired ends. During the incubation phase of change, a leader will bring together a critical mass necessary for change to occur. During the journey phase, the leader will guide that critical mass to shape the organization into a new way of being, a way that leads to the *maturity* of the organization. Changes fail for a lack of passion as well as a lack of speed during the transformation.

Layer Three–the Tensions of Leadership

Up to this point in the model's description, we have defined organizational agility by taking a look at what various leaders in the organization should be doing in order to produce the set of outcomes needed for future agility. It should be obvious by now that no one leader can achieve all of the outcomes needed to attain organizational agility. Every organization needs visionaries and stabilizers. Every organization needs negotiators and harmonizers. Because organizational agility involves the efforts of many within the organization, this model of leadership presents a unique opportunity to balance these styles and tensions of leadership. No longer does an organization need to reflect the style of one particular leader. Agile organizations find ways to incorporate many styles into the life of the organization, allowing leaders with differing styles to achieve success in differing parts of the organization.

Balancing these styles, however, is easier said than done. In order to detail what those balances might look like, we will now turn our attention toward the "how" of leadership rather than the "what" of leadership. I have listed below the tensions that must be balanced in order to maintain agility as an organization. Each outcome brings with it a natural, built-in tension. These tensions are named below, and expounded upon in the subsequent chapters.

Tensions Associated with the Ten Outcomes

Identity: Balancing the notes and the song
Vision: Balancing leadership and ownership
Mission: Balancing supply and demand
Results: Balancing progress and impact
Potential: Balancing participation and belonging
Performance: Balancing empowerment and accountability
Capacity: Balancing money and goodwill
Allocations: Balancing expenditures and investments
Passion: Balancing urgency and hope
Maturity: Balancing abandonment and creativity

A Few Final Introductory Remarks

Movement vs. Institution

This book is about developing movements as well as institutions. An organization cannot survive without some sense of structure and stability. Depending on the type of organization, some essentials must be in place to ensure the survival of the infrastructure itself, even if the infrastructure is altered. This book names those essentials in the outcomes. But, agile organizations are heading somewhere. Agility assumes movement. The purpose of becoming more agile is to be able to move in a new direction.

Organizations Are Organisms

This entire model is based upon an assumption that organizations are more like living organisms than machines. I believe that a living organism will always outperform a machine. Machines depreciate.

Organisms grow, expand, and develop. Organisms don't break. They slowly decay. Some die rapid deaths, while others are capable of surviving in a cancerous state for decades. Many organizations that once viewed themselves as well-oiled, well-running machines fall into the outmoded category today. Machines do not usually respond well to a changing environment. They rust, become obsolete, or are sold for salvage. When a machine breaks, we replace one of its parts. When a living organism is unhealthy, we focus on the total health of the organism in order to restore it. Unhealthy organizations are not in need of repair; they are in need of restoration.

Viewing a particular organization as a machine rather than an organism can tempt us to view the organization as merely the sum of its parts, yet an organization is not only *more* than the sum of its components, it is something *completely different* than the sum of its components. Every organization has its own identity, its own values, its own norms, and its own cultural manners. An organization is indeed a living organism, capable of growth and decay, celebration and mourning, joy and despair, change and resistance.

An Opening Pretest

Each chapter of the book begins with an opening test, encouraging the reader to reflect upon the particular organizational outcome prior to reading about it. At the end of each chapter, readers are encouraged to take the test again, incorporating their learnings from each chapter. In a similar manner, I invite you to take the following pretest, which encourages you to reflect upon the relative strengths of your organization, prior to reading about the organizational outcomes contained in this book.

Step One: You and every other person in your team (or you can do this exercise individually) will need ten 3x5" cards. Look at the list of organizational outcomes on page 13. As one person reads each outcome, place the name of the outcome on one of your 3x5" cards. As each subsequent outcome is read and described, place the cards in a rank order according the relative strength of each outcome within your organization. For instance, after you have written "identity" and "vision" on your first two cards, place the one that is currently stronger within your organization at the top and the other below it. Continue in this manner until you have placed all of your ten outcomes in descending order according to the relative strength of each outcome as it currently exists in your organization.

Step Two: Share your rankings with one other person.

Step Three: Seek to come to consensus with this person so that you end up with one rank order list between the two of you.

Step Four: Place the names of the ten outcomes on a sheet of newsprint and record each set of rankings on the newsprint in order to build the perspective of the entire group.

Step Five: Take a look at the results. Where do the majority of people in your team or organization believe the relative strengths are of each of the ten outcomes?

Step Six (*optional*): Seek to come to consensus as a group on the relative strengths of each outcome.

1

Embracing Culture: *Identity*

Identity——Vision
(strength)   (speed)

All organizations are known for something. Just as every human has a unique personality, all organizations have a distinct identity. Discovering your organization's identity will strengthen many facets of your organization, and strength is essential to agility. But, agility also requires succinctness. So, before you read the chapter below, take a moment to describe the identity of your organization in fifty words or less. Pretend that you are describing your organization to someone who has never heard of it.

Identity

In 2007, NBC aired a game show entitled *Identity*. Each show introduced twelve new mystery guests whose identities had to be correctly identified by the contestant. Any contestant who could identify all twelve identities in one hour by simply observing the clothes, postures, demeanor, facial expressions, reactions, and body language of the mystery guests won one million dollars.

For the next sixty seconds, let's play a version of this identity game. Picture your organization represented in one room along with eleven similar organizations. If you represent a congregation, picture eleven similar congregations. If you are reading this chapter with a classroom in mind, picture eleven other classrooms. Depending upon your organization, picture twelve parks, schools, service organizations, convenience stores, video rental places, etc. Further imagine that the contestant is chosen at random from your community. Could a member of your community correctly identify your organization by sight? Would it help if you were allowed to hold up a sign with three words that describe your organization? Which three words would they be? I will add one more component to make the identification easier. The game show host will choose a member from each organization represented on stage and grant the member sixty seconds to describe the corresponding organization. Your organization's representative can say anything about your organization except its name. Now, could a member of your community correctly identify your organization from the description of it from one of your members?

How well do you know the organization that you are leading? How markedly could you describe your organization in sixty seconds? Could all of your members describe it equally well? How long would it take you to get started? What props would you use? A motto? A phrase? A mission statement? A set of values? Might you sing a song, point to a poster, or distribute a brochure? What is the most similar organization to yours that you can imagine? Can you distinguish your organization from your neighbor? This chapter will help you add strength to your organization by clarifying its identity.

Uniqueness matters. Prospective members, customers, or volunteers like to know what you are all about and they don't want to read the newsprint from your last retreat or wait for you to pull a document off the shelf. They want to hear it from you and they want to know on the spot. Years ago, I interviewed a college president as part of a classroom assignment and asked, "What is the one thing that you cannot delegate?" "Articulating the identity and vision of this institution," he replied.

The president of an organization must be able to succinctly describe the identity of that organization. However, the real strength of an organization's identity lies in the ability of *any* of its members to describe it to an outsider, not just the president. My doctoral dissertation focused on the health of small, church-related colleges. One of the hypotheses that I was able to demonstrate with statistical significance is that the degree of agreement among the administration, students, alumni, and trustees regarding the distinctiveness of that college is one measure of its stability. The more people agree on the individuality of the organization, the stronger the organization will be.

A pastor can often articulate the identity of the congregation, but what about the other members? The chance of a prospective member asking the pastor rather than one of its members what the church is all about is actually very slim. Most newcomers first visit a church as a result of the invitation of a member rather than the pastor. Most prospective members of any organization initially interact with someone on the fringe of the organization rather than someone at its center, because those on the fringe usually have more contacts with others on the "outside." The pastor of a church, the director of a hospital, or the principal of a school each spends most of his or her time in that church, hospital, or school. People who want to know about the services that are provided, or the quality of the ministries, will usually ask one of the members at the edge. Thus, everyone in the organization should have answers to "What are you all about?" "Who are you?" "What is your identity?"

An organization has not fully embraced its identity until any member of that organization can easily articulate its identity to any member of its constituency.

The more that you and your members know about your organization, the stronger it will be. Identity is about building strength in your organization. Agile organizations know who they are so that they can better adapt to the world around them. Agility is *not* about succumbing to every customer's wish or copying the practices of your competitors. Agility is about knowing precisely who you are so that you will know how to adapt *without* compromising your beliefs and practices. By understanding your norms and your values, by knowing how you respond while at your worst and best, by knowing what storyline you are living out, you will gain strength and agility as a movement.

Getting a Handle on Your Identity

Remember that organizations are best thought of as living organisms. Your organization has character, personality, attitudes, growth spurts, and crises. Your organization had a birth and will eventually experience death as well as a multitude of transitions in between. Your church is a living organism. Your school is a dynamic entity. Your service organization has talents and strengths, weaknesses and shortcomings. It makes memories and it makes mistakes. Your organization has an identity apart from each of its members. Understanding organizational identity is more than a matter of identifying a few key elements within your organization. Organizational identities are every bit as complex as human identities. Thus, organizational identity is an ongoing, dynamic process.

Think of organizational identity work as similar to the dating process. In the beginning of any romance, couples ask "safe" questions of one another. They are on their best behavior. But, as time goes on, the questions become more serious and the information revealed more authentic. As a leader, you need to know your organization in order to better lead it and better describe your organization to potential suitors. Below, I list some categories of things that you should know about your organization, beginning with some basic information and proceeding toward the more complex. For each category, I provide a tool or process that I have found helpful for uncovering that category of information. But first, a word about conducting research on your organization.

Two Kinds of Research

When you conduct research about your organization, it is helpful to keep in mind that the results you obtain are absolutely dependent upon the method of study you choose. There are two main approaches to conducting research, *qualitative* and *quantitative,* and each carries its own benefits. *Qualitative* research helps to identify the *breadth* of the topic. Qualitative research methods include common practices such as interviews and focus groups, more casual methods such as observation and conversation, in-depth techniques such as naturalistic inquiry and thick descriptions, and more creative techniques such as "Storyboarding"[1] and "Asset Mapping."[2] Whenever a group has yet to discover the full range of the topic being studied, qualitative research is the more effective tool. In other words, if you do not already know the range of possible answers to your questions, qualitative research is your best bet.

The problem is that the primary tool that most people consider when they think about research is "surveys," regardless of whether it is the *breadth* or the *depth* of information that is preferred. Unfortunately, many people confuse the two methods by trying to understand the breadth of a particular topic using a quantitative survey, which seldom yields the desired information. For instance, adding an open-ended question to the end of a quantitative survey may sound like a good idea, but often does very little to expand the range of the topics already identified.

Surveys, along with instruments and other measures, typically fall into the *quantitative* category of research and reveal *depth* of information. Instruments are available that have been *validated* to prove that they are measuring what they propose to measure and have been shown to be *reliable* by measuring the same dimensions over time. Examples of these instruments include measures of church health such as "Natural Church Development" and measures of organizational culture such as the "Organizational and Team Culture Indicator." Quantitative methods help identify the intensity of the topic by revealing what percentage of the organization holds certain views or prefers certain methods. They show how many people are "on-board" or feel favorably toward a potential process. Qualitative methods add breadth. Quantitative methods add depth.

Research often involves the use of qualitative methods in order to identify the range of the topic and then quantitative methods to reveal how many individuals or members hold certain views and values within the identified range. For instance, an organization may use observation and focus groups to determine the range of values present within the organization and then conduct a survey to discover the relative strength of each of those values.

I will now describe a number of both qualitative and quantitative techniques that may be used to gain a better understanding of your organizational identity.

Safe Discoveries

Founding Story

Steven Sample writes, "An important asset for any leader to have as he works to inspire and motivate his followers is a credible creation story or myth for the organization or movement he's leading... [T]he real test is that such stories must appeal strongly to the leader's followers and to those whom he is trying to recruit."[3] Founding stories must be truthful, but that does not mean that there are not options in designing a founding story. In order to develop your founding story, scan the archives in search of a thread or posture that embraces where you would like to head in the future. Many organizations were founded to change something or to make a difference in the community. Find the niche in your historical narrative or the gem in your legend that supports your future vision. Show how you plan to meet the needs of your community–but in a slightly different way than your founders, because the needs of the community have changed since your movement first materialized over the horizon. Leaders will not be given permission to lead significant change until they have demonstrated an understanding of the history of the movement.

Members of Diana Schmiesing's second-grade classroom at Providence Elementary shape their understanding of history every year as they develop their own working constitution. They first study the meaning and benefits of rules and seek to understand why certain rules were included in our U.S. Constitution. They then apply those principles to their own setting, principles which usually include such items as "respect yourself" and "respect others." Identity formation does not end there. "For Schmiesing, teaching well starts with knowing each student really well: 'You have to take the time to know them and watch them.' She also has them keep journals."[4] Forming a new constitution or covenant of behavior is a way of building upon your founding story. Study how you came into being and then adapt that story into a behavioral covenant appropriate for your current context. Patty Trump, a teacher and friend of mine, uses a similar activity at Monroe Elementary School in Des Moines. Every classroom develops their own behavioral statement based on the school's "Monroe Pledge":

At Monroe we are people of character.

We are respectful.

We are responsible.

We care!

"I don't think you could find a single student who couldn't recite it correctly," Patty asserts. "When I have to confront students about their behavior, I always refer to the statement. Behavior is only acceptable if it complies with what we believe."

Norms

Every organization expresses certain expectations of its members. Your organization probably expects your members to dress within certain limits, express certain emotions more often than others, use a certain style of vocabulary, and arrive and depart at certain times. Some topics are encouraged while others are discouraged from appearing on agendas. Some organizations have a predominantly positive culture and others have a principally negative culture. Understanding norms can be a key component to identity building, but the process is not always easy to identify.

Many of the norms that exist within institutions are tacit. Extreme effort is often required in order to surface those norms, but the work comes with enormous payoffs. Often it is the more tacit norms that have the most influence upon an institution. For instance, a local church that maintains the unspoken expectation that every member will know every other member by name will have difficulty growing beyond a certain size. Other congregations who assume that people worship best in a quiet atmosphere will have difficulty appealing to the worship needs of people born after WW II. A regional judicatory that maintains the unstated expectation that every member congregation will agree on a controversial issue will have difficulty moving past the compliance stage of organizational development. Any institution that implicitly expects its members to have the same needs regardless of which generation they were born into will have difficulty involving leadership outside of its dominant generational group.

Unchallenged norms guide behavior in unnoticed ways. On the other hand, agile organizations regularly ask the "What if?" and "Why not?" questions. Tradition is a wonderful occasion for celebration, but never an occasion for administration. Performing tasks in a certain manner because that is the way it has always been done is a recipe for lethargy. Abandoning less effective methods for experimentation is a recipe for agility. Reaching down into the muck and mire and dredging up old traditions in order to either clean them off and embrace them or discard them as no longer useful is productive identity work. It is work that will strengthen your movement.

Values

Identifying the key values of your movement can be an effective tool for claiming identity. Richard Southern and Robert Norton describe a three-step process for identifying values of congregations, namely "(1) *Identify* those three to five values that are an essential part of the life and work of your congregation. (2) *Define* in writing exactly what each of these values means in the life of your congregation. (3) *Prioritize* them because they have varying degrees of importance and meaning in the life of your congregation."[5] Centering on a set of enduring values can have a durable impact on your constituents.

It may be helpful to consider key values as building blocks or linchpins in your organization. Often, an organization's distinctiveness will come from the way that those values are manifested rather than in the naming of them. Within every similar type of organization, the values that could be named are probably very similar. For instance, David Roozen suggests that the distinctiveness for religious denominations will come from one of the following: people, polity and structure, practices, or theology and purpose. He then suggests, "Any one of these possibly constitutive elements, not just beliefs or doctrine, can provide the linchpin of distinctiveness."[6] All denominations would probably list people, polity, practices, and purpose as sources of identity, but the tougher question to gain clarity on is, "What is it about each of those values that provides distinctiveness for us?"

Difficult Discoveries

The previous sections detailed aspects of identity that are somewhat safe in discovering and recovering. This section asks the reader to uncover portions of identity that can only be surfaced during more difficult times.

The Best and Worst of Times

So far, we have talked about identity formation work that will help you better understand your organization in everyday times. But, what does your organization look like when it is at its best? Its worst? Married couples can often recall their first argument or their first fight. That is because such an occurrence radically alters the environment. Can the relationship survive a fight? Can your organization survive a disaster? Think back. What does your organization look like at its worst? What tragedies have shaped your current identity? How does the movement respond?

In January of 2007, I was teaching a leadership class in which there were several Ohio State graduates and some spouses of current Ohio State professors. On January 8, 2007, Ohio State played the University of Florida for the national championship in college football. Although Ohio State had been ranked #1 the entire season and was the huge favorite, the team lost the game 41–14. As I walked into class the next day, I could see the dejected looks on my students' faces. With a son attending Ohio State at that time, I, too, was disappointed. I tried to capitalize on a teachable moment.

"Good morning class. It is indeed a tough day. Coach Tressel just called me and said, 'We are in a real jam here,'" I told the class, trying to elicit a smile.

"We certainly are in a tough place." I said, as I continued to fabricate a conversation with the coach. "You know, my strength is in my students, would you like for me to ask for their assistance in formulating a way through this?"

"Sure, that would be great, whatever they can do to help," I quoted the coach as saying. Students were beginning to buy into the manufactured setting.

For the next several minutes, we sought a way through for an institution that was in a very difficult moment. A school, known for its football prowess, had a lost a game that the world had expected it to win. We began by listing stakeholders:

- Parents
- Students
- Alumni
- Trustees
- The athletic director
- The president of the university
- The booster club

We then discussed how to respond to each specific group, seeking to frame for each constituent what had happened and to convince each eager listener that the school could move forward better than before.

One of the most helpful tools in framing the events from the day before was the tool of archetypes (described later in this chapter). I had just introduced that concept the day before and the students quickly put it to use. They concluded that Ohio State had been living out the "innocent" archetype, secondarily supported by a "warrior" archetype. The problem with both of these storylines is that they do not adapt well to surprises. In fact, the response from both of these is to work harder and continue in the same direction when faced with a crisis. I knew they were getting it when one of the students said, "Returning the opening kickoff for a touchdown was the worst thing that could have happened to Ohio State because it fueled their belief that this game was already in the bag."

Although merely an intellectual classroom exercise, it was interesting to see the real OSU story unfold in the days following the national championship game. Some of the students' perceptions and recommendations about how to deal with the loss came true while others did not. Still, we all learned more about Ohio State from watching the team respond to defeat than from watching another predictable outcome unfold. I imagine that the coach did as well. OSU began the 2006 season ranked #1 and never encountered a difficult moment. After their disappointing loss in the national championship game, they began the 2007 season ranked outside of the top ten. However, they fought their way up the rankings to show that they had been significantly underestimated in those early polls.

Just as with humans, we often learn more about organizations in the midst of tragedies than in the midst of everyday life. Observing organizational responses to shootings, suicides, tornadoes, and hurricanes helps us understand the strengths and weaknesses of organizations, even nations. For example, a *US News* article reported that Bush's downward approval rating spiral began the day after Hurricane Katrina.[7]

It is important to know an organization at its worst, but it also important to understand what your organization looks like at its best. "Appreciative Inquiry" is a tool that involves a four-step process of discovery, dream, design, and destiny, in which key stakeholders in an organization seek to identify what the organization looks like when it is at its best.[8] The real strength of this process lies in the dyad interviews that take place among the members of the organization. In a book entitled *Memories, Hopes, and Conversations: Appreciative Inquiry and Congregational Change,* Mark Lau Branson adapts the "Appreciative Inquiry" process for local congregations, recommending the steps of initiate, inquire, imagine, and innovate.[9] "Appreciative Inquiry" is an excellent process to utilize for institutions that have become so focused on the problems within their organizations that they can no longer see any positive approaches.

Image Branding

Cultivating a brand image can be a very powerful tool for identity formation. What brand image are you portraying to your constituents? What do your constituents think of your organization? Leonard Berry distinguishes among four different types of brand image.[10] The *presented brand* involves the image that you portray to others through your motto, logo, brochures, etc. This contributes directly to *brand awareness,* which deals with the recognition that your presented brand carries. How well are you presenting a positive, consistent image of who you are? *Brand meaning* includes both brand awareness as well as the experience that the person interacting with your organization has had. As you might expect, brand meaning is determined more by experience than brand awareness. Together, all of these influence the *brand equity* of an organization.

One of the newer techniques for building brand equity involves the use of "archetypes." An archetype assessment will uncover the "storylines" within your organization's culture. The architect of the tool, Carol Pearson, spent over ten years identifying the most common archetypal patterns in organizational cultures. Her list includes "caregiver," "hero," "sage," "jester," and many more.[11] Just as an organization that holds empowerment as a dominant value will differ radically from an organization that holds control as a dominant value, a "caregiver" organization will differ radically from a "hero" organization.

Uncovering the dominant archetypes within your organization can be a very powerful tool. "Young & Rubicam, Inc., a very successful and internationally recognized advertising agency, studied the fifty most successful brands in the world and found that they all had strong archetypal identities. The study also showed that the greater the fidelity the organizations had to their identities, the greater their Economic Value Added (profitability) and Market Value Added (stock prices)."[12] For instance, we can see the "lover" archetype, the storyline of "spanning the gap" or "building the bridge," in every Hallmark commercial. The power of the brand is that *every* commercial displays it.

I believe that the use of archetypes will become a powerful tool because it is an agility tool. Bridging the gap (lover archetype), overcoming the obstacle (hero archetype), or nurturing the one in need (caregiver archetype) can all take on many different facets as new needs and opportunities for organizations surface, while still maintaining the consistent brand image of the organization. For a list of individuals certified to help your organization discover its dominant archetype, contact the Center for Applications of Psychological Type.[13]

If You Are New to the Organization

If you are new to the organization and in charge of something, either the whole thing or just a part of it, do not hit the ground running without taking some time to understand the organization that you are leading. The chances of you running in the exact same direction as your followers by accident are very slim. The chances of you having an accident with your followers are much greater if you do not take the time to assess identity. Even if you have been promoted from within, you are now in a whole new position and must form new relationships with those on your team. Get to know the people. Either learn or relearn the identity of the group around you. Allow the roles of the team members to emerge. Listen rather than act, because it will pay dividends later: "Take the time to listen before you do anything else. You will set the tone; *and* it will be very difficult to reset it. If you start off by imposing your views on people, you're not going to have what you most need when you need it–namely, the commitment of the people you need to get the work done."[14]

Identity within Institutions and Movements

Identities among institutions and movements are often contrasted in sharp ways. Institutions often portray identity through their structures, their buildings, and their land holdings. Movements often portray their identity more organically, through their images, people, and impact. Static organizations are concerned about maintaining the institutional identity while movements are concerned about their direction. Some organizations have forgotten why they exist. Agile organizations not only know why they exist, they take steps toward their *raison d'etre* each day. Institutions tend to be comforted by the reality of familiar surroundings. Movements never wake up in precisely the same place as the day before.

Identities are also more adaptable in movements than institutions. As new people are added to a movement, as new and more effective methods are discovered, and as new ways of portraying and living out its identity surface, the movement changes each day. Institutions ask, "Will our constituents recognize us tomorrow?" while movements ask, "How do our constituents expect us to adapt to this new opportunity that we have discovered?"

Identity and Balance

Every organizational outcome presented in this book comes with a built-in tension that must be balanced in order for the organization to become more agile. Agile organizations not only balance strength and speed, they also maintain equilibrium on each organizational outcome by balancing coincident patterns with temporal patterns. With respect to the outcome of identity formation, the tension that agile organizations maintain is the tension between the *notes* of the organization and the *song* of the organization. Notes represent coincident patterns while songs represent temporal patterns. The "notes of the organization" are the patterns that it wishes to remain consistent over time, and more often include a subset of its beliefs, values, and norms. Your church holds beliefs that it never wishes to compromise. All organizations have certain "notes" that they choose to sing more often. All organizations possess favorite values, preferred norms, and visible beliefs. The notes give the organization consistency and stability. But, the notes of an organization must be balanced with its song in order for the movement to have mobility.

Ronald Heifetz suggests, "Thus, after hearing their stories you need to take the provocative step of making an interpretation that gets below the surface. You have to listen to the song beneath the words."[15] Songs are never sung the exact same way twice. The impact of a song depends upon who is in the choir, the tempo of the music, the accompanying instruments, the acoustics of the setting, the emotions of the singer, and the distance to the audience. Agile organizations find a way to sing the same notes to differing audiences in a different way in order to connect with each constituent group. Music styles of congregations change. School uniforms modify with emerging styles and trends. As members are added, as generations die, as trends surface, as opportunities arise, agile organizations learn to sing their songs in new lands. Agile organizations know who they are, but also recognize the need to adapt to the world around them. They learn to place their favorite notes in the songs of their constituency.

IDENTITY POSTTEST

Please take a moment to revise the description of your organization that you formed prior to reading this chapter. Refine your statement based upon your learnings and reflections.

IDENTITY DISCUSSION QUESTIONS

1. What are the first three words that come to mind when you hear the name of your organization?
2. What are the three most common emotions expressed in your organization?
3. What three people have been members of your organization the longest? What do they have in common?
4. What is your founding story?
5. What expectations does your organization have of new members?
6. What is there about your organization that people can only understand over time?
7. Recall a time when your organization was at its worst. How about at its best? How did those times differ from where your organization is today?
8. What image do you portray to your community? What image would you like to portray?
9. Complete the following sentence, "We the people of _____ _____, came together in order to form a more perfect _____."
10. What step have you most recently taken toward a new identity?

MEASURING IDENTITY

For the following list of items, please indicate the extent to which you believe that your organization currently demonstrates these behaviors and activities according to the following schema. As you answer the questions, please draw upon your personal knowledge of your organization during the last six months. Please do not be afraid to use all parts of the spectrum in your responses. Total the responses for your "identity" score.

5 = This is true of my organization almost all of the time
4 = This is true of my organization most of the time
3 = This is true of my organization about half the time
2 = This is seldom true of my organization
1 = I cannot recall a time when my organization did this

_____ We portray a clear and consistent identity.
_____ We understand why we were founded.
_____ We ensure that our members understand the key points of our history.
_____ We know on what we would risk our existence.
_____ We have an identifiable set of core values.
_____ We share a common understanding.
_____ We use charts and graphs to explain our history.
_____ The lives of our members are the best examples of our identity.
_____ We have adequate policies to govern our personnel.
_____ We have an overall philosophy of how we approach things.

Total the scores for your Identity total _____.

Total the scores for 1, 3, 5, 7, and 9 _____. This represents the extent to which your identity is contained in data, charts, and lists.

Total the scores for 2, 4, 6, 8, and 10 _____. This represents the extent to which your identity is housed in images, stories, and conversations.

2

Embracing Culture: *Vision*

Identity——Vision
(strength)   (speed)

Moving toward a vision can enhance every activity within an organization. Formulating a vision for the future and then allowing that vision to pull you toward that image will add speed to your organization. Speed is a key component of agility, but so is brevity. So, before you read the chapter below, take a moment to formulate a vision for your organization. Imagine that the next five years are the best years of its existence. In fifty words or less, describe your organization at the end of those five years.

Vision

A vision is a portrait. For organizations, a vision is a picture of the future. It is important for organizations to develop a picture of what they might become, given their identity. Take out a blank sheet of paper. Jot down everything you know about your identity. If you are reading this book sequentially, you should have several new insights about your organization's identity from the previous chapter. When complete, turn the paper over and draw an X on the other side. Then write the words, *You are here,* to symbolize where your organization is at the present moment. Now, take out a second blank sheet of paper and write the word *vision* on it. Crumple the paper with the word *vision* on it and throw it as far as you can. Pause for a moment. Then take a look at the ways that you have described your current organization on the other side of the "X." Given that identity, dream about a future destination represented by the crumpled paper on the other side of the room. What could you become, given your foundation, norms, beliefs, disposition, and brand image?

This chapter helps you imagine a future for your organization. Do not be concerned about your organization's shortcomings. You just threw a crumpled up piece of paper into the future rather than a sleekly designed paper airplane, and the reality is that the crumpled piece of paper probably flew further than a carefully designed paper airplane would have. Try it and see if you wish. Given your foibles and faults, strengths and strong suits, personality and preferences, what vision is possible for your organization?

Developing a Vision Statement

A vision statement is a description of a future desired state. A vision statement should describe what you desire your organization to become in the future and challenge your current membership to work toward it. It should not be attainable by the end of the week. A vision statement should describe your organization at some point in the future, perhaps three to five years down the road, and should lift up the natural result of living out the best of your current identity.

Developing a vision statement will add speed to your organization. The moment that you begin to envision a new future, members and staff begin to lean into that future. A vision statement is not a simple to-do list that can be ignored or about which to become lethargic. It is a statement about what the organization desires to be in the future, given the fullness of its gifts and opportunities. Vision statements inspire, motivate, and propel people into action. That is why "vision" is on the "speed" side of the balancing equation. Develop a vision and you add immediate energy to the organization.

Definition of a Vision Statement

Remember that organizations are best regarded as living organisms. Thus, a vision statement is a description of what your living organism could become in the future. Consider your current organization as being in its "teenage years" for a moment. For some readers, this will not be difficult. It is around the teenage years that the old tools of "lectures" and "grounding" fail to work. Teenagers don't want to be lectured or told what to do. Give them an ultimatum and they may just choose the least desired option just to assert their independence. Other approaches must surface. Employing the simple line from Dr. Phil, "How's that working for you?" is not a bad start. That often breeds some recognition that the current pathway has some shortcomings. Ask what other scenarios they may have already considered and encourage them to explore one of them, as they start down a path of imaging a different future that has real possibilities.

It might even work for your organization. We often describe adolescents as "having so much potential." We use even more specific language with teenagers whom we know: "Someday, I picture Mary or John as a research scientist, as an encourager of others, as an explorer, or as a great leader." Ruminate over your organization with the same emotion. Do the following types of phrases come to mind? "Someday I picture our organization as a model for others, fulfilling our call in creative ways, enticing others to become a part of our movement, because we are truly making a difference in the community." One aphorism that I live by is, "Treat adolescents like adults, but expect them to make teenager-type mistakes." It works with all types of adolescents, even organizational ones.

A vision statement should stretch the state of your current organization past the horizon it can glance up and see, but not past the breaking point. A vision statement should provide just the right amount of dissonance to inspire your organization beyond the present, but not so far that it breaks. Carefully crafted vision statements will help the organization take one new step each day toward that vision. They create such a yearning to become what is described that they create an automatic leaning toward the new vision. They literally help the organization pull in the same direction. But the vision is doing the pulling.

Vision statements may come in the form of a picture, a paragraph, a phrase, an image, or an icon. Vision statements are not as difficult to develop as some suppose. A vision statement is developed through describing an ideal future state based upon the identity of the present and the past. Thus, the first step involves reviewing where you have been. Timelines, histories, and recollections can all aid this process. "Appreciative Inquiry," "Asset Mapping," and "Future Search" are examples of processes that bring to the surface an understanding of current strengths and then invite the members to describe a desired future state. At some point, nearly every process I just listed puts the group of leaders in a room and asks them to hammer out a description of what the organization could become. In crafting the product, I find it helpful to use present tense language in describing an organization that obviously is not there yet, but could be, given the right amount of energy and focus. At this point, a few examples may help envision this product called "organizational vision."

Sample Vision Statements

Vision statements can be lengthy and give a complete picture of the future of the organization. Here is the vision statement for the American Baptist Churches, an extremely diverse, nonhierarchical group of congregations.

> American Baptists are a Christ-centered, biblically grounded, ethnically diverse people called to radical personal discipleship in Christ Jesus. Our commitment to Jesus propels us to nurture authentic relationships with one another, build healthy churches, transform our communities, our nations, and our world, engage every member in hands-on ministry, and speak the prophetic word in love.
>
> As a people of prayer, purpose, and passion, we are in the forefront of creating a diverse community of faith where people of every race, nationality, and culture gather as one in worship, witness, and work.
>
> The heart of the gospel is God's redemptive love. In our life together, the world will see the power of forgiveness to overcome alienation, the strength of love to transform hate, the power of grace to break the bonds of guilt, the triumph of hope over despair, and the victory of faith over doubt.
>
> Through the cross of Christ we embrace the world as neighbor. Our vision for mission energizes a multitude of servant ministries of evangelism, discipleship, leadership, new church development, social justice, healing, peacemaking, economic development, and education. Empowered by the Holy Spirit, we work together in mutual trust, humility, love, and giving that the gospel might be preached and lived in all the world.

Vision statements can also be short, comprising only one or two sentences in length. Here are a few samples.

From a local church: "We celebrate what Jesus celebrated and cry over the same circumstances that made Jesus weep. We follow Jesus wherever He leads, exploring pathways to discipleship for the 21st century."

From a judicatory: "We enable growth and health in every member congregation as we tackle missional needs beyond the reach of any single congregation and beyond the hope of any human thought."

From a hospital, "We address the physical, emotional, and spiritual needs of our patients, creating a synergism of healing and wholeness for each patient."

From a school: "We strive to understand the unique gifts of every student in order to inspire learning beyond any dream they could have dreamed when they first entered our doors."

From a consulting agency: "We deliver tailor-made processes that always achieve the desired results of our clients."

From a service organization: "We enable volunteers to use their unique gifts and collectively we abolish abuse in our community."

From a foundation: "We leverage forgotten resources in order to lift up forgotten people."

Mottos

Visions can also be delivered in the form of a motto. Mottos are only helpful if they provide a window to the vision. Several years ago I read a research report regarding state travel and tourism mottos and the conclusion was that none of the statements actually made the reader think of the specific state. "Wander Indiana," "Explore Tennessee" "Be our Guest in Texas," could all have interchangeable state names, thus none of them provided any information as to what is actually specific to that state.

Have you heard the phrase, "Can you hear me now?" Too many times? Maybe so, but what vision do you picture from that motto? Do you picture anyone, anytime, anywhere receiving a cell phone signal from a specific phone carrier? If so, then their motto provides a glimpse of their vision. Remember, visions have not yet been achieved, but do provide insight into the organization's hopes. What about, "So much is riding on your tires?" Getting the picture?

Functional mottos are not just catch phrases. They are "capturing" phrases. They capture our attention and force our view through a window portraying their vision.

Fill in the Blanks

Envisioning comes naturally for some and not so naturally for others. Some work well with a blank sheet of paper. Others are better at refining or revising material. For those interested, I have provided a *fill in the blank* vision statement below:

We are a group of _____ individuals, setting standards of _____, creating an environment of _____, known for _____, admired for _____, and sought after for the _____ manner in which we deliver it.

(For the sake of integration, below I have repeated the statement, this time including suggested categories from the identity chapter):

We are a group of _____ (*values*) individuals, setting standards of _____ (*when we are at our best*), creating an environment of _____ (*norms*), known for _____ (*founding story*), admired for _____ (*service or product*), and sought after for the _____ (*brand image*) manner in which we deliver it.

External Inputs

In developing a vision, it may also be appropriate to include information external to your organization. This type of work is known as environmental scanning. Even though your organization has an identity as unique as a person's fingerprints or facial expressions, sociological trends tend to affect most organizations. Awareness of these trends and the incorporation of them into the identity of the organization can enhance the agility of the organization. A lack of knowledge of the world around it can severely limit an organization's ability to respond or even understand the needs and preferences of the constituency. At this point, this is simply a reminder to include external as well as internal information in developing a vision. For a list of some current trends potentially affecting today's organizations, please see chapter 9.

Teams, Retreats, and Summits

Peter Koestenbaum suggests that the content of visions comes down to thinking big and thinking new.[1] As you contemplate the future of your organization, it may be helpful to gather an envisioning team. Vision statements are often best developed apart from the daily routine of the organization. Retreats and summits are effective tools for developing vision statements. Simply removing people from their traditional settings can greatly enhance the type of thoughts and conversations that take place among them.

Ronald Heifetz encourages leaders to create a holding environ-ment[2] for effecting adaptive rather than technological change, and creating new visions that will guide the organization to new heights, which certainly falls on the adaptive side of change.[3] Many organizations find it helpful to create an envisioning team to both develop a new vision statement as well as guide the implementation of such a statement. Place people on the team who can think beyond any single issue that may be facing your organization. It is also helpful for the team to represent the full range of diversity within your organization. This will make it more difficult for them to get on the same page initially, but will absolutely produce a better product in the end.

Not a Mission Statement

The best vision statements do not come in the form of a list. Lists lead to mission statements, while pictures, phrases, and images lead to vision statements. An organizational vision is a picture of the future based upon current and historical identities. A vision is a picture of what the organization might become in the future, given its current realities. A mission statement depicts what the organization should be doing, while vision is about becoming.

Multiple Visions

How many visions do you need? Have you ever considered developing more than one vision statement? You may be thinking that more than one vision statement might lead to confusion, but the reality is that agile organizations have multiple visions because they are able to focus on more than one area simultaneously. When most organizations think of developing a vision, they ponder a new vision for the organization itself. But what about developing a vision for all those who intersect with your organization? If you are primarily a service organization, begin to ponder how people served by your organization will become different as a result of your service to them. What is your vision for those whom you serve? Schools, seminaries, and training programs should have a vision of the type of graduates they might produce. If you are a business, what is your vision for your customers? Do you expect your customers to be qualitatively different as a result of using your product? Will they be happier? Will life be easier? Will they be more fulfilled?

What future do you dream for your staff or your employees? How do you expect your staff to become different people as a result of working or volunteering within your organization? As a congregation or service agency, do you strive to affect your community? If so, do you have a vision for what your community might become? Are you environmentally friendly? How does your vision include that notion? Visions are pictures of the future. You may need to develop more than one picture to capture all of your dreams. Below, I discuss three types of potential visions, based upon three types of stakeholders that exist in nearly every organization.

Stewards–the founders, investors, and representatives, including governing boards

Served–intended recipients of the organization's products or services

Servants–full-time, part-time, and temporary or volunteer staff of the work team

A Vision for the Stewards

The stewards of an organization are those who care for or are responsible for the welfare of the organization. If a board of directors governs your organization, they are the stewards. If stockholders govern your organization, they are the stewards. In a congregation, the members themselves may serve as the stewards or the stewards may reside in a presbytery, a council, or the office of a bishop. The stewards of an organization are its decision makers. What future do you envision for the stewards of your organization? How will this group of people grow as a result of caring for your organization? Will they be more mindful of the needs of your community as you seek to address them? Will they better understand the trends that are affecting organizations such as yours? Will they become more knowledgeable or more astute? Will they become better decision makers? Are relationships important among this group? Will they create a sense of community among themselves? In addition to developing a vision statement for your organization, it may also be helpful to develop one for stewards.

A Vision for the Servers

Developing a vision statement for those who serve within the organization may also be beneficial. Describe how you envision them becoming different people. What will they learn, how will they grow, what will they become as a result of being a part of your movement?

What is your vision for those who serve in your congregation, your school, or your agency? Develop that vision and then monitor its progress among your servants.

A Vision for Those Served

Finally, it is also imperative to develop a vision for those served by your organization. For a religious movement, developing a vision for those served by your congregation, judicatory, or nonprofit often becomes the heart of your vision, for these groups exist to serve others. How do you envision those whom you serve becoming different as a result of your service to them? What are you offering them? Will they become more purposeful, more connected, more comforted, more compassionate, or more committed? Organizations who can articulate their vision for those whom they serve and then live out that vision can have an enormous impact of the lives of those persons.

Vision within Institutions and Movements

Many institutions possess vision statements and yet lack speed. For a vision statement to add speed to the organization it must drive decision-making processes. If a statement must be pulled from a file cabinet, opened on a computer, turned to in a book, or brought into the room from a phone call by a support staff person, it will probably slow down the organization. Visions statements only have power when they have influence in the organization. The only thing worse than not having a vision is having a "shelved vision." Underutilized vision statements are worse than nonexistent vision statements. With no vision, at least there is a sense of a need for something. Shelved vision statements send the signal that the future is irrelevant to current activities.

Another necessity for a vision statement to add speed to an organization is that the organization must view itself as part of a movement. Even institutions must have a sense of movement in order to be affected by a vision. By definition, visions statements challenge an organization to move from point A to point B. They inspire it to become more. They pull an organization toward a new reality. As we will see in a later chapter, maintaining the *status quo* requires a similar amount of energy as moving toward a new vision. Institutions determined to maintain the *status quo* will not be inspired by a new vision because they require change. On the other hand, institutions that see themselves as part of a movement need a vision to inspire them toward the new future. Movements are headed somewhere and the vision provides the destination.

Moving from point A to point B does not necessarily involve a physical move. Sometimes the grandest moves involve a change of heart or change of attitude rather than a change of location. A formerly static organization that acknowledges the need to be on a journey takes a great stride merely by its acknowledgment of the need for change. The first step toward a new vision is often the most difficult. Organizations must concede to the requirement of movement in order to actually move toward a destination.

Have you ever driven a car without power steering? They still exist. We own a 1990 Ford Ranger with no power steering. The key to turning it is to already have it moving somewhere. Friction on the pavement is a prerequisite to turning. In fact, it would be easier to redirect it in the right direction if it were moving in the wrong direction than if it were absolutely stationary. That last sentence may be worth rereading. Some organizations lost their power steering long ago, presumably from lack of use. For those organizations, advancement is also a prerequisite to turning in a new direction. It may be necessary to get the institution moving in the wrong direction, but moving nonetheless, before moving it in the right direction. Visions get organizations going. As people begin to dream about new ideas, new possibilities, and look toward new horizons, they stand up and begin to stretch and move around a bit. It will take concerted effort to actually coordinate their actions, but at least they are stirring. Visions help institutions see themselves as part of a movement, and visions do not work without movement.

The Power of Vision

Melinda Davis suggests that one of the reasons why visions are so powerful is: "Reality itself has gone mental. The future, you might say, is all in your mind."[4] She provides ample evidence that the scale has been tipped from what we can experience as immediate and real toward what occurs in our own heads. We talk to people whom we cannot see more often than we talk to them face to face. People communicate through text rather than face to face. Cookies on our computers provide more important information to marketers than the words we type. People work with the imaginary more than with the hands-on. "At one time, two-thirds of working Americans earned their living by making things, Henry Ford style. At the beginning of the twenty-first century, two-thirds earn a living by making decisions."[5] Because visions also occur in our heads, they are powerful tools for the culture in which we live. Visions capitalize on the means of the day. The best ones bring images to the surface and stir emotions within us. They deal with our heads and hearts, not just our hands and feet. The language of visions speaks to the motivations in our minds.

Vision and Balance

Agile movements not only balance strength and speed, they also maintain equilibrium on each organizational outcome by balancing coincident patterns with temporal ones. With respect to vision, the tension that agile organizations maintain is the tension between visions that subsist only in the mind of the leader versus visions that live in the hearts of the people. The natural tension for vision lies in balancing leadership and ownership.

Articulation of vision is a task that should never be delegated. People apart from an organization never fully trust new directions that do not originate from the center of the organization. Discussions about new directions, new ventures, new acquisitions, release of property, change of logo, or change of senior staff are never trusted unless they originate from the leaders or trustees of the organization. Even when an organization is clearly frustrated, floundering, or failing, if the center is silent, it is as if the organization is silent. Vision cannot be delegated away from the center. New visions are articulated from the center out, or at the very least information flows through the center before it goes out to the whole. Any other scenario breeds mutiny, schism, and blocking. Visions must survive in the mind of the leader.

On the other hand, we have all known visionaries who could see a future, but not describe it, let alone motivate anyone to move toward it. Visions that reside solely in the minds of the leaders will never gain traction. Effective visions gain an increasing percentage of membership affinity at every stage. Visions may surface from an individual, but survive only in groups, and thrive only by gaining ownership throughout the organization. Developing ownership of a vision is crucial to its implementation.

The three keys to building ownership are portraying, listening, and adjusting. Once a vision has any form to it at all, it should be portrayed to the members—who are asked for their input—and then adjusted according to that input. Building ownership of a vision is a cyclical process. As the vision gains ever-increasing detail and the circle of feedback is continuously widened, ownership is built. However, the balance must occur. Visions must be articulated from the center and then receive ownership from every direction.

VISION POSTTEST

Please take a moment to revise the vision statement description that you penned prior to reading this chapter. Refine your statement based upon your learnings and reflections. You may also want to write three separate visions: one for the stewards, one for the servers, and one for those whom you serve.

VISION DISCUSSION QUESTIONS

1. Is your current organization acting more like a child, a teenager, a young adult, a middle-aged person, or a senior adult?
2. What is the best compliment that your organization has ever received?
3. Recall a motto that you may have seen on a billboard or heard from a recent commercial. Can you guess what vision they were seeking to portray?
4. Distribute your most recent news publications. What vision would people perceive based solely upon these documents?
5. Who are some people who might form the foundation of an envisioning group for your group or organization?
6. What is your vision for the stewards of your organization?

7. What is your vision for the servants of your organization?
8. What is your vision for those served by your organization?
9. Do you agree that it is important for an organization to be moving, even if in the wrong direction, rather than not moving at all? Can you identify any examples of movement that need to be redirected or realigned within your organization?
10. Is your current vision contained more in the minds of your leaders or the hearts of your people?

MEASURING VISION

For the following list of items, please indicate the extent to which you believe that your organization currently demonstrates these behaviors and activities according to the following schema. As you answer the questions, please draw upon your personal knowledge of your organization during the last six months. Please do not be afraid to use all parts of the spectrum in your responses. Total the responses for your "vision" score.

5 = This is true of my organization almost all of the time
4 = This is true of my organization most of the time
3 = This is true of my organization about half the time
2 = This is seldom true of my organization
1 = I cannot recall a time when my organization did this

_____ Our leaders portray a clear vision.
_____ Every person in our organization understands our vision.
_____ Our leaders demonstrate what the organization can become.
_____ Members gather together to discuss vision.
_____ Our leaders can easily describe our vision.
_____ Everyone gives input into our hopes and dreams.
_____ Our leaders believe in our vision.
_____ Asked on the spot, any member could tell you where we are headed.
_____ We have a visionary leader at our center.
_____ Our members tell our vision to anyone who will listen.

Total the scores for your vision score _____.

Total the scores for 1, 3, 5, 7, and 9 _____. This represents the strength of your leadership to articulate your organization's vision.

Total the scores for 2, 4, 6, 8, and 10 _____. This represents the extent to which the people own your vision.

3

Embracing Purpose: *Mission*

Mission——Results
(strength)　　(speed)

MISSION PRETEST

Mission matters. Businesses must decide what business they are in. Nonprofits must decide what mission to embrace. Both must prioritize their narrowly defined missions from the full range of activities capable of consuming their organizations. Defining the mission of your organization will add strength to your organization. Strength is a key component of agility, but so is leanness. Describe the purpose of your organization as concisely as possible. Write a mission statement for your organization as you now understand it in fifty words or less. Even if you have an official mission statement for your organization, please write this one in your own words.

Mission

What do you think of when you hear the word *mission?* Consider some recent popular phrases that include the word *mission...*

"What is your mission in life?"
"Your mission, should you choose to accept it..."
"How many missions did you complete in the military?"
"Mission impossible?"
"Mission accomplished!"

The word *mission* comes from the Latin *missum,* meaning "sent." Mission involves "sending," "going," and "doing." The previous chapter dealt with the development of a vision for your organization. This chapter deals with mission. There is a clear distinction. Vision is about picturing. Mission is about prioritizing. Vision assumes a futuristic perspective. Mission begins with today and moves forward. Vision pulls. Mission pushes. Mission does and delivers, competes and completes, accomplishes and achieves, explores and executes.

The word *mission* is ubiquitous in our language, and yet everywhere it is used, it contains a common thread. Mission is always about getting things done. The 1986 British film entitled *The Mission* tells the story of a Spanish Jesuit priest, Father Gabriel (Jeremy Irons), who enters the South American jungle to build a mission and convert a community of Guaraní Indians to Christianity.[1] The mission of *The Mission* was to do things—"to build" and "to convert." *Mission Vao* fought battles as a Star Wars character. As a record label, *Mission* provided an alternative format to the mainstream. Spacecrafts accomplish *missions.* Organizations have mission statements that typically focus upon getting things done. There is actually a town called "Mission"—several, in fact. They exist in Kansas, Oregon, South Dakota, and Texas—plus one in British Columbia whose stated mission is to welcome new visitors and investors and improve the quality of life for its residents. There is also a school called *Mission College* in Santa Clara, California, whose mission is to do things, more specifically to:[2]

- Create a student-centered institutional culture of professionalism, discovery, inclusion, and success
- Shape the academic program to meet community needs, emphasize student learning, and foster instructional excellence
- Promote academic success and create dynamic, innovative student services programs that address the richness of Mission College's student population and community

- Raise institutional standards by developing the potential of the Mission College community and providing the tools necessary to foster innovation, responsiveness, and excellence

Are you getting the picture? Mission is about doing things. Visions help organizations imagine what they could become, while mission statements help them narrow their range of activities in order to achieve that vision. Mission and vision are both imperative as well as discrete. Psychologist Jonathan W. Schooler pioneered research in the area of verbal overshadowing and has shown how simple tasks such as describing a person actually inhibit our ability to recall a picture of that same person. "Your brain has a part (the left hemisphere) that thinks in words, and a part (the right hemisphere) that thinks in pictures, and what *can happen* when you describe a face in words is that your actual visual memory is displaced."[3] That is precisely why organizations need both mission and vision. They come from two different sides of the brain and two different sides of the organism known as an organization. Visions help us picture a future. Mission helps us plan a pathway to get there. Both are necessary motivators for organizations.

Mission is more than a random list of potential organizational activities. Agile organizations don't just do things for the sake of being active; they do the right things, the most appropriate things, the preeminent things. They focus upon the tasks that they are best prepared to accomplish and are most needed by their constituency. Agile organizations are narrowly focused and outcome driven. Clumsy organizations are slow to react, bogged down by too many possibilities, and worn down from being pulled in too many directions. Agile organizations understand that the range of what they could be doing is always much broader than what they choose to do. They choose the superlative thing from the many right things to do and track movement toward their goals. As you might imagine, over the years a number of tools have surfaced that can help an organization define and focus its mission, but first I need to ask what type of organization you are leading. The answer to this next question may have a profound effect upon the development of your mission.

Sodality or Modality

Is the institution that you are leading a sodality or modality? A local church is a modality. So is a school. The municipalities of Mission, Kansas, and Mission, British Columbia, are modalities of the same type. On the other hand, a service organization is probably a sodality.[4] So is a parachurch organization. "Modality is represented in the Bible by the church in Jerusalem and the church in Antioch, the church in Ephesus and the church in Rome; and in history by the parish church and the community church... The sodality is represented by Philip the evangelist and Paul and Barnabas; by the medieval friars, the Catholic orders, Protestant missions, and Christian aid agencies."[5] Your local church would be a modality, but "Bread for the World" would be a sodality. Is this concept beginning to make sense? A modality carries with it certain expectations and limitations. The most notable limitation is usually geography, and the most notable expectation is usually the formation and maintenance of a sense of community, though all modalities carry additional expectations.

Let me demonstrate the impact of being a modality a bit further. Imagine your local church announcing that it is no longer going help people connect to God, grow in their faith, foster community, or hold worship services anymore in order to focus all of its energies on feeding the hungry. How would you respond? "Are we still a church?" might be your reaction. Indeed, at that point, the church would cease to be a modality and would become a sodality. Imagine your local school announcing that it is no longer going to teach via the classroom and that it is going to abandon the teaching of math, science, and social studies in order to focus entirely upon reading. At that point it, too, would become a sodality rather than a modality. Modalities and sodalities are both necessary. Yet modalities can never compete with sodalities with respect to focus, and sodalities can never compete with modalities with respect to contact with members.

Herbert Simon[6] pointed out nearly fifty years ago that imposed expectations have little if any motivating power and should be viewed as constraints rather than motivators. I have added evidence to his theory over the years by comparing a list of reasons people give as to why they attend their local church with a list of stated reasons as to why their church exists. The two lists often have little in common. Thus, for a modality, certain pieces of mission, such as evangelism and discipleship, will be mandated, but may not be automatic motivators. Dealing with a set of imposed expectations will limit an organization's ability to focus as narrowly as it might want. On the other hand, it can easily compensate for this detriment by capitalizing on the sense of community that is built into the organization. Churches must recognize the potential power of gathering their members together on a weekly basis, and schools must recognize the potential power of having students and teachers relate to one another on a daily basis. The opportunity for relationship building in such environments is incredible. Modalities have relationship built into their DNA, while sodalities have purpose built into theirs.

Mission within Institutions and Movements

Institutions are called to carry out their historic purposes: purposes that are written into their charters, purposes that are expected of them by their constituents, purposes that many times their ancestors suffered for promoting. Living out those purposes is honorable, just, and commendable. Carrying out those expectations, however, requires a certain amount of infrastructure to maintain. Because so many expectations are mandated for modalities, modalities will naturally have more infrastructure than sodalities, and thus will carry a much stronger temptation to become purely institutional rather than a movement. The problem surfaces when the people leading those infrastructures focus more on the structures themselves than on the purposes those structures are called to address. Schools that pass laws benefiting teachers over students, churches that expend the vast majority of their budgets on their members rather than their community and their world, judicatories that focus more on regulating rather than resourcing clergy are all heading toward organizational demise caused by institutional myopia. The problem is not that they have an institutional structure; such structures are necessary for modalities. The problem is that they have lost their first love.

Because of the emphasis upon community, one of the dangers of modalities is that they are places where people gather, not just organizations that do mission. Overemphasizing the gathering, the committees, and credentialing of leaders to lead the infrastructure and the training of meeting facilitators to carry out meetings rather than engage in mission can lead to becoming over-institutional. "[T]his view of the church as a 'place where certain things happen' located the church's self-identity in its organizational forms and its professional class, the clergy who perform the church's authoritative duties."[7] Again, fostering community is not a bad thing; indeed, it is mandated by being a modality, but the sense of community should be seen as a means to accomplishing mission, not just an end in itself.

Any institution that focuses more on survival than on its mission is on a downward spiral. Growth of the institution's resources is a byproduct of accomplishing its mission. Modalities such as schools, churches, and judicatories that focus solely on maintaining the institution rather than on their mandated expectations are destined to live and die in the institutional realm. Churches, schools, and judicatories that wish to thrive must become missional again. They must be intentional about being missional and work toward becoming a movement. Movements deemphasize structures and overemphasize their mission.

Purpose–A Rallying Point

All exceptional activity has a purpose. The entire mission of your organization needs a rallying point. The development of your mission will usually include several key activities to focus upon in the future, but all of those activities should come under a broad purpose. Activities need a thread. The description of that thread forms the mission statement for your organization. Articulating your mission often involves finding that thread that cuts across several components of your organization. Jim Collins suggests that the ultimate mission of an organization occurs at the intersection of three items:[8]

What are you deeply passionate about?
What drives your economic engine?
What can you be the best in the world at?

Mission Statements

Putting the mission of the organization down into a single concise statement can greatly enhance the ability of the members to recall and operate within the defined mission of the organization. The organization's mission statement should be a declaration of its ultimate purpose. John Carver suggests that mission statements contain the following set of characteristics:[9]

1. Results terminology
2. Succinctness (they are memorable and quotable)
3. Authoritative generation
4. Horizontal integration (they foster cooperation with other groups)
5. Vertical integration (they are applicable at every level)
6. Ubiquity (they should appear everywhere)

Ultimately a mission statement defines the broad purposes of the organization and provides a rallying point for all constituents.

Vision Gives Rise to Mission

Vision and mission are connected. If you have already articulated a vision for your organization, your vision can serve as a springboard for your mission statement. For example, if your vision pictures every member of your community as having a home or shelter, then your mission statement will probably include providing affordable housing, short-term shelter, and diversified housing in your community. If your vision includes an image of every member of your congregation being a mature disciple, then your mission statement will probably include providing multiple discipling opportunities for people of all ages and at all stages of faith development. If you have a vision to become a conference center of excellence for your judicatory, then your mission statement might be, "Provide unparalleled hospitality to our guests, maintain the grounds and accommodations, and offer resources to enhance the purpose of every group who steps on our grounds." The development of a mission statement can become an answer to the question, "What must we do to achieve our vision?"

Developing Mission Statements for Modalities

If you are leading a modality that is a part of a family of institutions (such as a local church, a judicatory, a camp, a school, a hospital, or a town), certain expectations will be associated with that modality that you cannot ignore, expectations that extend even beyond the building of community. In addition to fostering a sense of community, people expect churches to worship, to educate, to care for their needs, and to reach out to the needs of others. In addition to enhancing social skills, people expect schools to teach, to foster self-esteem, and to develop good citizens. Sometimes these expectations are codified in the charter or incorporation papers of the organization. But even if they are not, they are real expectations that cannot be ignored. That is why so many mission statements for modalities look the same. I will show how to overcome this dilemma.

The mission of a modality will naturally be broader than the mission of a sodality, but it still must be articulated succinctly and inspirationally. When the CEO of a sodality entitled, "Specks and Spectacles" responds to the question, "What does your organization do?" by answering, "We provide eyeglasses for underprivileged children and adults," there is an immediate satisfaction with the answer. On the other hand, when a local church pastor responds to that same question by saying, "We worship God, we help people grow in their faith, and we seek to meet the needs of people in our community," the inquirer is likely to respond with, "Tell me something I didn't already know." For a sodality, the key to developing a mission statement is to succinctly state your purpose. For a sodality, that is enough because the purpose is not intuitively obvious. A modality must go beyond the statement of the obvious.

Modalities have four options in developing compelling mission statements:

- State the obvious in a creative and abstract manner
- Overemphasize one aspect of your modality
- Emphasize something extra, beyond the obvious expectations of your modality
- Focus more on the "how" and the "whom" than on the "what"

I will illustrate the four options listed above for a local church whose expectations of being a modality are to worship God, disciple people, meet human needs, and promote the gospel. The examples stem from churches with whom I have consulted. An example of the first option might be, "Upward, Inward, and Outward," or, "A ministry for all people and all people for ministry," or, "We connect Sunday to Monday." An example that overemphasizes one aspect of the modality functions, such as the evangelistic aspect of being a local church modality might be, "Reaching the lost at all cost." Two examples that fall into the third category of emphasizing something in addition to the modality functions are, "Growing one handshake at a time," and, "Come for the food, stay for the fun." An example of the fourth option, which emphasizes the *whom* and the *how* over the *what*, is, "We bring the hope of God to the neglected of our community through the transformation of neighborhoods."

In developing a mission statement for a modality, the challenge is to find creative and inspiring ways of stating and accomplishing its purposes, and to be recognized as distinct from other similar modalities. The challenge of developing a mission statement for a sodality is to avoid becoming overspecific and too short-term oriented, so that the mission statement will have life and vitality beyond the current year or the current set of emphases. In any case, purpose, rather than survival, must be the rallying point for the organization.

Additional Tools for Mission Development

As you can imagine, a number of tools have been developed over the years to help organizations develop and define their mission and purpose. I briefly describe two of these tools below.

SWOT

One of the more common and enduring tools for mission development is called SWOT. This is a process that seeks to identify the "Strengths," "Weaknesses," "Opportunities," and "Threats" currently facing your organization. Strengths and weaknesses refer to what the organization does well and what it does not, but SWOT goes beyond that. Strengths can also refer to positive assets within the organization that include people as well as money. Weaknesses identify the gaps that may exist within your organization. Weaknesses can also refer to missing skills or assets.

Just like individuals, sometimes the weaknesses of an organization lie opposite its strengths. For instance, if following protocol is a strength of your organization, flexibility may not be. If camaraderie is a strength, welcoming others may not be. All organizations will have both strengths and weaknesses.

Strengths and weaknesses point to components within the organization, while opportunities and threats look outward. What unique opportunities lie outside of the organization? Is there a housing development going up nearby? What new businesses are being launched that offer potential partnering? Is a new school or a new assisted living center being built nearby? What traffic patterns are changing or what roads are being built that may have an adverse affect on your congregation? How will the failed school levy affect your church or your business? Many pastors choose to become involved in the local Chamber of Commerce or a service organization in order to stay abreast of the opportunities and threats within the community.

Below are some categories that you may want to include when doing a SWOT analysis:

Promotional capabilities
Range of services
Similar organizations
Ability to respond
Ability to expand
Ability to obtain rapid feedback
Skills of staff and volunteers
Team spirit, mood of membership
Coordination of effort
Experience
Quality of services
Facilities and equipment
Financial leverage
Operating leverage
Balance sheet ratios
Personnel guidelines
Membership turnover
Staff turnover
Staff and volunteer satisfaction
Leadership development

Positioning

In the early 1980s, Michael Porter popularized a radical concept in the strategic management world, namely the idea that "only a few key strategies, known as positions in the marketplace, are desirable in any given industry."[10] Porter suggested that for any grouping of similar organizations there exists a limited number of strategies that organizations within that grouping should logically embrace. In the business world, for instance, B. D. Henderson suggested that there were only four possible positions for any new product, namely: (1) star (high potential and high market share), (2) cash cow (high market share, but low growth potential) (3) problem child (high growth potential, but low market share) and (4) dog (low potential and low market share).[11] Porter suggested that "being all things to all people was a recipe for strategic mediocrity and promoted one of three positions, namely, cost leadership, differentiation, or focus."[12]

While Porter's Competitive Strategy model was an immediate hit with businesses and many service organizations, it is only in recent years that the Competitive Strategy model has become applicable to congregations, because the model assumes that similar businesses or service organizations compete in the delivery of their products or services. In an era of high denominational loyalty, congregations merely had to name their denomination for mobile loyals to seek out their preferred denominational congregation and join it. But, as we are keenly aware, that level of denominational loyalty has dramatically faded. But, since the consumer model has arrived in most communities, much competition exists, even among congregations, making Porter's model worthy of consideration.

Porter's concept also assumed that businesses or organizations embracing the positioning model desire growth, expansion, or improvement, an assumption consistent with agile organizations. Thus, let's apply it to congregations. Consider the following possible types of strategies for congregations desiring to grow, expand, or improve, rather than simply maintain their current level of ministry and membership:

- Narrowing your focus by targeting a particular group of people for inclusion and adapting staffing, services, and programming to meet the needs of that group
- Broadening your focus by seeking to include additional generations or ethnicities through changes in worship, programming, process, and symbols

- Maintaining programming, but marketing or advertising a unique aspect of your existing identity to your community
- Adopting a new vision and mission and transforming your congregational resources, systems, and structures to achieve the new vision
- Emulating the worship and programming of a desired congregation such as a megachurch by networking with other churches of that type
- Wiping out your existing traditions and bylaws and creating a new entity in the old facility

Obviously, there still exists the possibility for great variety within each strategy. For instance, two congregations may adopt the first strategy of targeting a particular group of people, but design very different worship styles and programs by choosing different targeted groups. Two congregations who choose to better market their existing identity may differ significantly if one chooses to market its political advocacy and community organizing role while the other chooses to market its ability to develop small support groups. However, there are a limited number of strategies from which to choose for a congregation, judicatory, service organization, etc.

I have included the type of internal strategy required to achieve the desired position in the marketplace, such as adapting programming, marketing, or networking. Many organizations would like to adopt a particular position, but are unwilling to make the kind of internal changes required to achieve such a position. Others adopt a strategy that does not fit the desired position. Still others place all of their energy into one outcome while abandoning the other issues discussed in this book. "Crash and burn" stories abound in which a local church pastor has attended a church growth or church renewal conference only to return, announcing a new vision for the congregation. Such an announcement ultimately fails because the leader ignores all other components of organizational development. Remember that agility not only requires strength and speed, but also balance.

Prioritizing

No matter whether you currently lead a congregation, a judicatory, a school, or a service organization, eventually you will need to narrow your list of possible activities in order to become more agile. Being pulled in too many simultaneous directions often bogs down organizations that seek to be all things to all people all of the time.

So, at some point, the leaders of the organization must embrace a prioritization process in order to focus the current mission of the organization. Such processes usually contain similar essential steps:

- Preparation
- Brainstorming
- Narrowing
- Commitment

The various processes differ according to the emphasis placed upon each component as well as the number of people involved, but nearly every mission development process contains these components. I briefly describe each component below, offering some options for each one.

Preparation

During the preparation phase, the leadership of the organization must "prime the pump" by persuading the members to begin to think creatively. In a service organization, the director might distribute a series of articles or memos highlighting the best practices of similar organizations. In a congregation, the pastor might preach a sermon series highlighting New Testament practices that would stretch the current activities of the congregation. In a school, the principal or superintendent might host a series of continuing education events for the staff, helping them think beyond their current classroom activities. A team of leaders might design a curriculum aimed at exploring new possibilities for an envisioning group, a staff, or a collection of small groups to enhance outward thinking. The leadership should also reinforce the identity and vision of the organization, as described or developed from suggestions in previous chapters of this book. The goal of the preparation phase is to help as much of the membership as possible to be able to easily and quickly raise to the surface new ideas during the next phase of brainstorming.

Brainstorming

I prefer to involve as many people as possible in the brainstorming phase. Invite the entire congregation, school, staff, or constituency to a retreat for the purpose of uncovering new mission possibilities to achieve the vision of the organization. Such an invitation obviously requires some advance planning, but can often be accomplished with less work than originally conjectured. If the entire membership is invited, I suggest that such an event be held on the grounds of the existing organization if possible, in order to make it easier for people to get there. If the leaders do the brainstorming, it is always best to go to a different location. The retreat should begin with a re-articulation of the current vision and a brief message from the leaders highlighting the current identity.

With people gathered in a common setting, primed for brain-storming, turn them loose and watch the energy escalate. Certain ground rules for brainstorming should be stated, such as not critiquing anyone else's suggestion, sharing air time among the participants, and including as much diversity as possible within each small group. Round tables work best for such activity. Make sure to record each idea on newsprint, small blocks of paper, or 4 x 6" cards, but do so in such a way that each idea can be posted or reported for all to consider. Most people underestimate the time required to fully engage each member during the brainstorming phase, but I suggest allowing a minimum of two minutes per person per question asked in order to get to the more creative responses—which typically do not surface during the first round of conversation. It is also helpful to give a minute or two of silence for those who process internally prior to asking people to respond verbally either as a whole group or in small groups.

Narrowing

While the preparation must be done in advance of the retreat, ideally, the brainstorming, narrowing, and committing will all take place in one setting. After the newsprint or cards full of ideas have been displayed around the room, give people time to read every suggestion displayed. I usually suggest conducting this activity over a snack or meal break. Encourage people to read each comment and reflect upon its possibility. Encourage people to make notes and chat with others, but try to prevent any caucusing of like minds that might curtail individual expression.

One of the best and most efficient methods of narrowing the plethora of ideas is through "dot voting." Purchase several Avery® dots in advance, or you can simply use markers if you trust people to use only the allotted number of votes assigned. Ask everyone to place a dot next to the ideas that they most like at this stage of the process. The facilitator will need to combine any duplication of ideas, but this can be done fairly quickly with everyone standing and giving input while walking around the display. If there is an argument over whether or not to combine two or more ideas, the originator of the idea has final say in whether or not there is indeed duplication. Once you have your set of possibilities ask people to mark or place their allotted number of dots on the ideas they like the best. This allows ideas that are simply too outrageous to drop from the list without hurting anyone's feelings via critique. I usually suggest giving each person multiple votes, approximately two votes for every ten items displayed. Tally the votes and announce the results, which are already visible to the full room of participants.

Commitment

If feasible, I suggest seeking a certain level of commitment from the participants prior to departure. This can range from the formation of small task forces that begin working on each priority identified, to seeking broad consensus from the group for the items receiving the most votes. If the brainstorming and narrowing have taken place in one setting, the commitment level is fairly easy to achieve because people usually perceive a level of fairness about the process that has led to certain items rising to the top. But, there is still much more power in *seeking* commitment to the items that have surfaced rather than *assuming* it.

Follow-up

Even though the participants will have committed to embracing only a certain number of priorities following the retreat, every idea generated should be recorded. I encourage distribution of the full set of suggestions rather than merely those that rose to the top. Transparency always builds trust. If task forces have already committed to certain priorities, track the results. If broad consensus is the only product, then the list of priorities should be handed over to an envisioning group, executive committee, or governing board for further discussion and distribution to departments.

In the months following the retreat, all agendas, budgets, scheduling, and time management should radically reflect the results of the retreat. One of the most controllable pieces in an organization is the agenda at meetings. Typically the chair or key staff set the agendas with input from others. Agendas should continue to explore the resources, personnel, and potential volunteers necessary to embrace the priorities, in addition to foreseen obstacles. Ownership should continue to be broadened at every stage by asking key groups and individuals, "Here are the priorities that have surfaced so far. In your opinion, are we getting it right?" Portraying, listening, and adjusting should become a constant feedback loop.

Sample Mission Development Retreat Outline

Below, I have included a sample outline for a mission development retreat.

Opening Session

- Describing our modality or sodality (description of key expectations)
- Celebrating our identity (description of current identity)
- Embracing our vision (description of current vision)
- Results of SWOT analysis (strengths, weaknesses, opportunities, threats)

Brainstorming Session–Sample Questions

- Imagine it is five years from now and we have fully achieved our vision. How did we accomplish that? What did we do that was new and different?
- What else could our organization do to please or honor God?
- How could we more fully utilize our strengths?
- How might we better respond to the opportunities around us?
- How could we better live up to our potential?

Narrowing Session

- Post each idea around the room
- Combine duplicated items
- Give each person two dots per every ten items posted
- Ask people to place their dots on the items that might best advance the organization's vision and purpose
- Record the votes for each item
- Announce the results

Commitment Session

Form new self-selected small groups of four to six people around the items with the most votes

Ask each group to respond to the following questions:

- What will it take to make this happen?
- Can we list some goals and objectives?
- Who else needs to be involved to build ownership?
- What organizational changes would help make this happen?
- Where in our existing structure could progress be monitored?
- What could we measure to see if we are heading in the right direction?
- Are there any limitations for the implementing group to recognize?

Mission and Balance

Remember that every organizational outcome presented in this book contains a built-in tension that must be balanced in order to maintain agility. For the outcome of organizational mission, all organizations must balance what they can supply with what the customers and constituency are demanding. Defining mission is about prioritizing. However, agile organizations achieve a balance between what the organization has to offer and what its constituents need.

All organizations must discover what they can *supply* to the world. Seldom does an organization discover a rich need for something that it already has in abundant supply. More often, resources must be adjusted, recruited, repackaged, reengineered, and combined in order to meet the needs that surface. Needs that match what the organization can supply must then be marketed. Bringing the supplies and demands together is often a constantly developing process as cohort groups shift, geography changes, and transitions occur. Emphasize too much on the supply side and an organization will grow obsolete. On the other hand, overly emphasize the demand side and an organization will falter from over-promising and under-delivering.

Many congregations fall into the trap of over-emphasizing the supply side. Consider a congregation that boldly proclaims, "We offer the saving grace of Jesus Christ" to a single mother who is simply looking for affordable, respectful daycare! The young mother may not yet be able to focus upon the rich benefits that will be accrued from new life in Christ until she finds someone who can meet her immediate need. Encouragingly, daycare is one of the ministries that has a strong potential for attracting new members. Congregations must assess the needs of the community before they can realize just what needs to be offered that they indeed can supply.

MISSION POSTTEST

Please take a moment to revise the mission statement that you drafted prior to reading this chapter. Refine your statement based upon your learnings and reflections.

MISSION DISCUSSION QUESTIONS

1. Why does your organization exist?
2. What are the top three priorities for your organization in the next three months? The next year? The next five years?
3. What would it take to accomplish your vision?
4. Is your organization a sodality or a modality?
5. What are the major strengths and weaknesses of your organization?
6. What are the major threats and opportunities facing your organization?
7. Is your organization "well-positioned for the future"?
8. How well are you balancing what you can supply as an organization with the needs of your constituency?
9. How memorable is your mission statement?
10. How well does your recent agenda reflect your mission statement?

MEASURING MISSION

For the following list of items, please indicate the extent to which you believe that your organization currently demonstrates these behaviors and activities according to the following schema. As you answer the questions, please draw upon your personal knowledge of your organization during the last six months. Please do not be afraid to use all parts of the spectrum in your responses. Total the responses for your "mission" score.

5 = This is true of my organization almost all of the time
4 = This is true of my organization most of the time
3 = This is true of my organization about half the time
2 = This is seldom true of my organization
1 = I cannot recall a time when my organization did this

My organization...

_____ has a clearly defined set of priorities.
_____ is driven by the needs of those outside the organization.
_____ takes time to identify its unique capabilities.
_____ has a clear understanding of the needs of its constituents.
_____ decides how to approach tasks before doing them.
_____ exists for outsiders.
_____ knows what is has to offer.
_____ knows the needs of our community.
_____ is well positioned among similar organizations.
_____ is fully aware of the threats and opportunities facing it.

Total the scores for your mission total _____.

Total the scores for 1, 3, 5, 7, and 9 _____. This represents the extent to which your mission emphasizes what you can supply to your constituents.

Total the scores for 2, 4, 6, 8, and 10 _____. This represents the extent to which your mission emphasizes the needs of your constituents.

4

Embracing Purpose: *Results*

Mission——Results
(strength)   (speed)

RESULTS PRETEST

All organizations produce results, but not all organizations focus upon the results of greatest potential impact nor celebrate those results in an effective manner. Producing and celebrating key results is an important component of agility and will add alacrity to your organization, as initial results often lead to more significant and long-lasting results. Demonstrating results also draws outsiders inside your organization to discover how you operate. Thus, it is imperative to track key indicators and advertise your results well. So, before you read the chapter below, take a moment to describe the five best indicators that will reveal how well your organization accomplishes its purpose during the coming year. At this point, do not worry about how easily the indicator can be tracked or measured, just list the best ones.

Results

Results add an immediate sense of speed to an organization. Achieve something through cooperative efforts and the accomplishment adds confidence, energy, pace, and hopefulness to the team. Results breed results. Yet it is amazing how many capable organizations do not chart or celebrate their results with their constituents. Sometimes, there is a sense that "everyone already knows" about the results. Humility can also surface as a reason for "results resistance." Yet it is essential that organizations share their results with their current members as well as their potential members. Carver asserts, "The only justifiable reason for organizational existence is the production of worthwhile results."[1]

Celebrating results motivates a team to work hard on days when results seem distant. Take, for example, this metaphor. On a lightly breezy day in the summer, look at some trees. The longer that you look at the trees, the more you notice that the tops of trees are in constant motion from some gentle wind, but if one looks only at lower branches, there is little indication of movement. Organizations are often like that. Not everyone is aware of movement, of stirrings, of winds affecting another part of even the same organism. So, results must be shared and celebrated with vigor at all levels.

Indicators

During the results pretest at the beginning of this chapter, I asked you to list the five best indicators that would reveal how well your organization embraced its mission at the end of the year. Indicators provide answers to the questions:

"How will you know if you have done well?"
"How will you know if you have made a difference?"
"How do you know what you have achieved?"
"How did this year compare to other years?"
"What will have changed in people's lives if we truly embrace our mission?"

Sample Indicators

Below, I have listed some sample indicators for different organizations:

Sample Indicators for a Local Church:
- Membership change
- Worship attendance
- Small group attendance

- Number of people actively involved
- Dependence upon God
- Worship vitality
- Quality of ministry in the various workplaces of members
- Mission involvement
- Mission giving

Sample Regional or Judicatory Indicators for Denominations:
- Number of congregations
- Membership percentage change of each congregation
- Mission giving
- Number of people trained
- Effectiveness of training
- Satisfaction of pastors
- Number of congregations networked together

Sample Public School Indicators:
- Proficiency scores
- Student attendance
- Student satisfaction
- Teacher attendance at in-service days
- Teacher satisfaction
- Parental involvement
- Use of experimental curriculum
- Number of staff involved in advanced degrees

Sample Service Organization Indicators:
- Satisfaction with services delivered
- Number of new services added and abandoned
- Morale
- Strength of brand image
- Donations
- Mailing list
- Budget
- Percentage change of endowment

Independent and Dependent Variables

Before I talk about how to measure the indicators that you have named, I would like to describe two types of variables. Just as understanding the difference between quantitative and qualitative research can help one in understanding how to gather information, understanding independent and dependent variables can greatly enhance the formulation of results. A variable is something that can change—such as an attitude, or a test score, or one's satisfaction with a service provided. The theory of independent and dependent variables suggests that by adjusting certain variables (called independent variables) we can influence other variables (called dependent variables).

Typically, we seek to influence several independent variables (such as classroom environment, fear of the subject matter, attitudes toward the school, variety in instructional methods, etc.) in order to influence one dependent variable (such as test scores of students). This theory is a myth because if the test scores do improve, this will in turn loop back and affect the students' attitude toward the subject and school, so not only will the independent variable influence the dependent variable, but the dependent variable will in turn influence the "independent" variables as well. In addressing this problem, some researchers measure *correlations* between the two variables and avoid the cause and effect hypothesis altogether. The other reason that this is a myth is that it is impossible to control for everything that may affect a student's ability to learn or test well while making adjustments to certain other independent variables, such as what they watched on TV the night before, how much sleep they received, or whether or not they liked what they ate for breakfast on the day of the test. In order to combat this problem, researchers try to control everything else that might possibly influence the dependent variable, which as you can imagine is not easily done.

However, if you keep in mind that the model is not perfect, that everything in an organization is connected somehow and that it would probably make more sense to talk about loops than straight lines of cause and effect, the theory of independent and dependent variables can be a useful concept to embrace especially when discussing organizational results. It is indeed possible to influence a dependent variable by influencing other independent variables, even though we may never pinpoint the independent variables that caused the change in the dependent variable.

Lead and Lag Indicators

In applying this concept of independent and dependent variables to organizations, Paul Niven has suggested the use of the terms "lag indicators" and "lead indicators."[2] In his model, lag indicators serve as the dependent variables and lead indicators serve as the independent variables. He defines the lag indicators as "outcomes of actions previously taken," hence the term "lag." The proposal is that these indicators will lag behind the others as the lead indicators influence them. Furthermore, Niven encourages all organizations to track four types of lag indicators:

- Customer Satisfaction
- Financial Indicators
- Employee Learning and Growth
- Internal Organizational Processes[3]

Take a look at the five indicators that you named in your pretest. Have you heard the commercial about people deciding what friends to include in their "favorite five"? Consider your top five indicators as your organization's favorite five. These indicators will narrow your focus even more than a mission statement by converging your efforts and your timeline. Convergence will add speed as your organization moves toward a destination. Think of this piece as removing all resistance as you enter the wind tunnel. It is impossible to achieve the full range of your mission statement in one year, so you must divide it among your "favorite five."

Chances are that the majority of your five indicators are lag indicators rather than lead indicators, which means that you will have some additional work to do in tracking and measuring. Again, a lead indicator is a variable that you can influence directly, but a lag indicator is a variable that you can only influence indirectly. For instance, in a local church, membership and attendance are lag indicators. It is impossible to influence these factors directly. After all, you cannot go out on the sidewalk and drag people into your organization. People must be invited. They must somehow hear from someone else about your congregation. They must want to become a part of it. All of these activities lead up to the person becoming involved. Advertising, marketing, inviting, and welcoming are all lead indicators for the lag indicators of membership and attendance.

Take a look at the indicators again. Have you identified at least one indicator in each of the above categories suggested by Niven: customers, finances, learning, and processes? For instance, have you identified a financial indicator such as budget, endowment, or mission giving? Have you identified a satisfaction indicator among those whom you serve? Have you identified a member development indicator such as faith development or growth in skills? Finally, have you included an internal process indicator such as worship, education, or volunteer recruitment? If you are new at this, I suggest naming one indicator in each of the above areas and stay with that particular indicator until the organization has made a significant difference on that factor. Once achieved, you can then add a new indicator. In this way, your organization can maintain a balance in its emphases upon the financials, customers, employees, and processes. Indeed, the original model is called "The Balanced Scorecard."[4] Robert Kaplan and David Norton developed the original model and Niven adapted it for nonprofit and government organizations.

There are also other excellent tools available to track results similar to the Balanced Scorecard depending upon your type of organization. Phillip Schlechty suggests the following set of standards for schools, which are a good set of indicators: (1) input or contextual standards, (2) process standards, and (3) outcome standards.[5] Do a Google search of the field called "metrics" along with your type of organization and you will discover other such resources.

Let's further explore the idea of lead and lag indicators. If you do have any lag indicators in your list of five, the next step will be to identify several lead indicators for each lag indicator since you cannot directly influence your lag indicators. Let us take the example of membership again. Imagine that you are a church or service organization that believes that increasing membership would be one of the key indicators of whether or not you had achieved your mission during the coming year. Some sample lead indicators for membership might be:

- Number of guests who visit each week
- Number of follow-up phone calls, letters sent, and visits made to visitors
- Number of invitations extended from existing members
- Number of special events held specifically targeting guests
- Number of dollars spent on advertising
- Number of segmented marketing tools used
- Number of hits on your Web site

Each lag indicator should have three-to-five lead indicators associated with it. The expectation is that influencing the lead variables will positively affect the lag variable. If an increase in the lead variables, however, does not lead to an increase in the lag variable, then I suggest one of three options: (1) try to discover what or who else in the organization may be inhibiting or working to decrease the lag variable, (2) adopt a new set of lead variables, or (3) adopt a new lag variable for a period of time, and perhaps returning to the old lag variable at a later time. All variables should be reviewed on at least an annual basis. Of course, any indicators that were influenced in a positive direction should be celebrated, but the beauty of this model is that there is nearly always something to celebrate. If the lead indicators were chosen with care and assigned to capable leaders to provide oversight of them, there will nearly always be positive movement on the lead variables. Even if positive movement on the lead variables does not lead to movement on the lag variable, at least you know what does not work in the organization, and chances are that the lead variables led to positive changes somewhere in the organization if not on the targeted lag variable. As you begin to positively impact one area of the organization, watch for positive improvements even in unexpected places.

Results within Institutions and Movements

Movements measure variables that track involvement with the outside world. They tend to overemphasize results that speak to making a difference among the customers and constituents. Institutions tend to track variables that strengthen the internal components of the organization. An organization too focused upon maintaining its institutional status will focus too heavily upon internal results.

Members of institutions also tend to take one another for granted. One way of helping institutions begin to adopt a customer or constituent mentality is to encourage them to view the internal departments of the institution as customers to one another. Everyone in an organization has customers, even the maintenance crew and accounting department. Their customers may be internal to the organization, but tracking results indicators among these departments, such as customer satisfaction and goodwill, will enhance constituent focus throughout the organization. Organizations tend not to measure interactions between components that have no choice but to relate to each other, such as two internal departments. But Rod Napier suggests, "Whenever customers cannot elect to go elsewhere, measurement is essential."[6]

Encourage every department or division to assess what is deemed to be important by those whom they serve. Measurement of the satisfaction of those served internally is at least equal to that of those served externally because we have no other means of knowing if the internal customers are satisfied. Is there a way to tell what people being served value without polling them? Yes. Typically, all customers value reliability, responsiveness, confidence, and empathy from those serving them.

Many nonprofits shy away from "customer" language. One of the myths is that customer information does not apply to the nonprofit world or to religious organizations, because they do not produce a "product." However, more than 86 percent of people in the United States work in the services sector, where focusing upon those served is even more important, because value is created in real time as relationships are built.

Qualitative and Quantitative Variables

All variables can be measured, but some can be measured more easily than others. Anything that you can count, known as a quantitative variable, is usually easier to measure. For instance, you can count dollars raised and dollars spent, attendance at big events and attendance at feeder events, the number of people involved in an activity, etc. You cannot count attitudes, learnings, or feelings; but you can measure them in a more qualitative manner. For instance, if you are seeking to measure people's satisfaction with a service or an event, you can simply ask them how satisfied they were on a certain scale that describes the high and low points of the scale. Doing this consistently will track satisfaction over time. For many qualitative variables, such as attitudes, aptitudes, strengths, skills, and beliefs, someone may have already developed a valid and reliable instrument to measure what you are seeking to measure. Discovering such instruments is easier than it may seem. It may merely involve a trip to your local college or university, library, or marketing agency.

Formulas

As I mentioned earlier, the discipline that tracks results in organizations is known as the field of metrics. The field uses the same principles outlined above to track variables of influence and variables of indication. As you begin to track the results of your organization, you will surely make mistakes in both identification and measuring, but remember that the field is not perfect. Even doctoral dissertations contain several pages showing the "limitations" of the particular research study. Because we live in a world of such abundant choice, people want to know what difference you are making as an organization. If you want to attract people, you will need to somehow reveal your results. If you have a phobia to statistics, learn to trust someone who may help you track results. A statistician could quickly develop a regression formula in order to ascertain the best predictors for any indicator identified by your organization as important. The concepts remain the same even in sophisticated studies. What changes is the complexity of the tools.

Strategy

At this point, it may be helpful to introduce "strategy" into the conversation. If vision provides the "where" and the mission indicators provide the "what," strategy provides the "how." Strategy is about matching. Strategies match items, people, purposes, and destinations. Strategies match internal components to external components; they match specific achievable goals to desired outcomes; and they match the internal strengths of the organization to environmental needs.

Goals and Objectives

Goals and objectives are perhaps the oldest form of strategy. They are yet another form of independent and dependent variables. Objectives are designed to achieve preestablished goals. Achieve the objectives and the goal will be met. Objectives break down a larger goal into more manageable components. The smaller objectives should include funding, people, resources, and activities. Objectives outline what it will take to achieve the goal. One of the best definitions of planning that incorporates not only the concepts of goals and objectives, but also introduces conditions, resources, activities, impact, and rationale is the following: "A project responds to a set of conditions by gathering resources that support activities that produce results that have an impact on people, and a rationale explains why this is so."[7] For more on any of these concepts, please read Kathleen Cahalan's book *Projects that Matter*.[8]

Alignment

Once you have identified your favorite five indicators with their supporting cast of lead indicators, someone will have to take responsibility for working on them or nothing will get done. The best plan in the world is worth nothing if no one implements it. Each indicator should be assigned as the responsibility of one person. Even if it takes more than one person to influence one of the indicators, only one person should be given specific responsibility for it. "Just one person?" you may ask. *Yes.* Allow me to elaborate. The only choices other than the number one are less than one and more than one. It is not a good idea to assign the same indicator to more than one person. As long as a person has a reasonable expectation that someone else may be taking care of something, then the person will let someone else be responsible for it. If less than one person is assigned responsibility that would, logically, be zero, which is also the level of output you can expect on any indicator to which no one is assigned responsibility. Most organizations are fraught with good, noble activity. If it were a matter of suggesting that people give up their unhealthy, undesirable, and unwanted activities in order to embrace the newly developed favorite five indicators that your leadership team just concocted, the task would be easy. The leadership must motivate people to take on this additional responsibility, or hopefully replacement responsibility, and give up something else that they probably have grown accustomed to doing well. That will not happen by the power of suggestion. Each indicator must be assigned to someone who will be responsible for tracking it and who will be asked about it. Assigning the indicators to staff members assures that individuals within the organization are focusing upon the essentials of organizational purpose. All other planning should be done around these core indicators.

The concept of "assigning" indicators to individuals should be interpreted loosely here. In an ideal environment, a team of people would actually select the indicators for themselves. The key is to ensure that someone is responsible for each indicator. Hopefully, the one responsible will have passion for the item allocated.

Assigning each indicator to one person is the first step of organizational alignment. If the alignment process goes no further, you will have accomplished more on this mark than most organizations. Ideally, alignment will go beyond the development and assignment of the lag and lead indicators. Ideally, every single division or department within your organization will be able to locate its particular passion in your mission statement as well as the indicators chosen to represent those missional activities. If a department or an individual cannot see himself or herself in the mission statement, then either the mission statement is too narrow or the organization is too large. Ultimately, the alignment piece involves ensuring that every department's passion is aligned with the purpose of the organization. If you have the time, ask each departmental unit in your organization to specifically describe how it is contributing to your overall mission by beginning with the areas about which it is most passionate.

Execution

Once responsibility for each results indicator has been assigned to someone, expect each person to carry out his or her new responsibility, and give words of encouragement along the way. Typically people will accept encouragement on what to do or how to do something, but not both. Assigning tasks to a group of people counts as a "what." Let them figure out the "how." If people need help on how to approach something, they will probably ask. More mistakes are made limiting people's activity by putting a fence around their approach than by giving them too much freedom to carry out a strategy. The person assigning a responsibility to someone else is often "wired" in an entirely different manner from the recipient. What may make sense to one person might be foreign to the other.

Think twice when telling someone else to do something your way. The correct manner in which to delegate is to jump in with one foot and leave it there. Most leaders jump in with both feet (by not only describing the task but telling others how to do it) and then just as abruptly remove both feet (by abandoning the unit and assuming that it will be done in the manner described). Delegation is much more an art than a science. The best delegators assign tasks to others in a manner that allows for the task to be done in an even better manner than it would be by the one who assigned it.

People assigned an indicator should be responsible for two things: tracking the variable and influencing the variable. Certain information will be forever lost if not gathered at the appropriate time. Gathering information usually involves planning ahead. For instance, if customer satisfaction data is not gathered at an event via a feedback form, it may be unrecoverable. Second, individuals responsible for indicators should be given some leeway to make adjustments. For instance, the person responsible for welcoming guests should be encouraged to ask for new resources to be developed as needed or more volunteers to be recruited if necessary to accomplish the task. Adjustments should be encouraged to enhance the indicators along the way, but do not abandon the indicator altogether even if something initially appears not to be working. Sticking with the plan is a matter of trust: "If an organization's strategic focus and business priorities change, it will never earn the trust of those who work either within the organization or with it. Leaders take note: they too must keep their strategic focus and business priorities steady in order to be trusted."[9]

Leverage Points

Up to this point, I have encouraged the adoption of multiple indicators in order to achieve the broadness of the organization's mission. Indeed, if the activity of one of your major departments or divisions is not reflected in your stated purpose, you should either abandon that department or alter your mission statement.

In this section, however, I emphasize the power of specificity in your mission by encouraging depth as well as breadth. Remember, agility also includes balance. Leonard Berry suggests that the key to organizational effectiveness is being simultaneously focused *and* entrepreneurial. In describing such balanced organizations, he writes, "These companies are innovative on both the strategic and execution levels, that is, adding new activities and improving the execution of existing activities. The desire to be the best in their chosen business runs deep and compels internal change."[10]

Several authors have recently written about the power of naming a key activity that could serve to transform the organization if embraced by everyone in the organization. Michael Hammer and James Champy call them "cross-functional integrations."[11] Thomas Bandy calls these activities "opportunistic initiatives," defined as "the ability to seize the moment, create and liberate mission teams, and surf the chaos of change."[12]

I call these potential actions "leverage points." Below, I describe several others' interpretations of this concept.

Thematic Goals

Patrick Lencioni offers an exception to the long-term nature of mission statements by suggesting that thematic goals can also serve as short-term rallying points, providing further sources of organizational purpose in order to avoid people working in silos. He defines a thematic goal as "a single qualitative focus that is shared by the entire leadership team–and ultimately, by the entire organization–and that applies for only a specified time period."[13] Some of the indicators listed above could serve as a thematic goal for the organization, although the development of a thematic goal for the entire organization usually requires a bit more creativity. For instance, imagine if "uplifting worship" became the goal of an entire congregation and was emphasized not only at the scheduled weekend worship services, but also at every meeting, every event, as well as in people's personal lives? Or imagine a congregation practicing "discernment day," in which every member covenants one day a week to make every decision only after consulting God's wisdom on it. Or imagine if the concept of the "question behind the question"[14] became the focus of your entire service organization? Or ponder the notion of the "second right answer" (the idea that the "first right answer" may be acceptable but not compelling) being adopted throughout an entire school system?

Provocative Propositions

Ludema and others in the "Appreciative Inquiry" movement call these leverage points "Provocative Propositions." The criteria for a provocative proposition include:[15]

- Is it provocative–does it stretch and challenge?
- Is it grounded–is it realistic?
- Is it desired–do you really want it?
- Is it stated in affirmative and bold terms as if happening now?

One example of a provocative proposition is a high-technology company in which human resources staff "sit in as full partners with their line clients during key strategy sessions. Line managers receive such timely, rapid, and on-target support that they invite input from their HR consultants, not only on HR issues, but on a wide range of general management concerns."[16] Provocative propositions rise out of discussions about what an organization looks like at its best and what it could become if its "best" were the basis for all other activity.

Catalytic Mechanisms

Jim Collins calls these leverage points "catalytic mechanisms" and sites "short pay" as an example, in which Granite Rock allows a customer to pay after the service has been rendered and pay less than the full amount if they deem that the service warrants it.[17] Another classic example cited by Collins is 3M's "15 percent rule" in which employees are actually required to devote 15 percent of their time to research and development activities.[18] A similar example can be seen in the University of Chicago, which was founded without departmental walls and can boast more Pulitzer Prize–winning faculty than any other university.

Patrick McKenna suggests, "It's all about striving, and struggling, for something noble, uplifting, and inspiring. Work with your group to articulate your compelling challenge, realistic or crazy, and pursue it. Be outrageous. Be the group that everyone talks about."[19]

The Governance Role in Producing Results

Regardless of who is assigned the responsibility of tracking and influencing results, a group of people shares the fiduciary responsible for ensuring that the results occur. The role of a board of directors is to define the identity of the organization, adopt a vision for its future, set the mission priorities, and hold the staff accountable for achieving results that fulfill its purpose: "Worthwhile results always relate to the satisfaction of human needs. Whose needs, which needs, and what constitutes 'satisfaction' are the unending, subjective quandaries of a board. Resolving the important, even existential value dilemmas inherent in these questions is the very heart of leadership governance."[20] Boards set policy. Staff is responsible for carrying out those policies. That does not mean, however, that the board cannot help in the achievement process. Most organizations require well-functioning working teams that extend beyond staff to include board members and other volunteers in order to achieve their mission. A large portion of a board member's time may be spent working side by side with staff and others to achieve one of the named indicators. When this happens, it is important for both the staff person and the board member to recognize that they have removed their other hats and are now working as a team with no titles assigned to any individual. This keeps directors and staff from confusing their roles while in the midst of a project.

Results and Balance

Once leaders have been able to focus the mission of the organization, people will immediately expect to hear about results. Many leaders are adept at setting goals, establishing objectives, designing programs, and hosting events in order to demonstrate *progress* toward the defined mission. Leaders show progress by illustrating how the organization is advancing toward its goals. But, along the way, leaders must make sure that the goals adopted are the right goals. Are the goals truly having the desired *impact?* Many organizations have planned themselves right out of existence by driving hard to achieve the same set of irrelevant goals that were adopted for a previous generation of constituents or consumers. Goals must be verified regularly to ensure that they are making a difference. On the opposite end of the spectrum, many high-impact organizations have met their demise from a failure to demonstrate to their board members or donors any progress on the goals adopted by that board. Thus, in producing results, all organizations must balance progress and impact.

Sometimes, organizations can actually impede progress by overstating or understating impact. For example, the historic argument over whether to focus upon mastery learning or the needs of the exceptional and special students is a dilemma that shows up at all levels of education. In a recent article from the Chronicle of Higher Education, Laurie Fendrich laments about how the focus upon metrics is destroying the quality of higher education: "While what's currently practiced as outcomes assessment may have a place in the fields of mathematics and the hard sciences, it's a destructive blunderbuss when applied to the arts and humanities."[21] One of the problems that Fendrich experienced when volunteering to serve on an outcomes-based committee within her university was that the metrics she experienced (based upon customer satisfaction of current and former students) were deemed as not objective enough to fulfill the standardized demands of those wanting "progress." Forcing every student to show progress in only a couple of areas limited the impact of her teaching on the entire classroom. I believe that such demands fall too far on the side of progress while actually impeding impact. It certainly is appropriate to expect results in an organization. But the demonstration of those results should be flexible enough to incorporate progress, impact, and the methods employed.

In demonstrating results, organizations must balance progress and impact. Listen carefully and you will hear people clamor for both. Certain personality types demand to hear how objectives have been met and goals achieved. Other types long for narrative stories of how individual lives have been altered by the efforts of the organization. It is not easy to achieve both, but when accomplished, a balanced approach can leave the constituent with a strong sense of satisfaction. As a parent of a graduating high school senior, I attended a nonprofit annual meeting for an organization entitled, "Call to College." The mission of the organization is to raise funds for student tuition. During their annual meeting, the organization appropriately reported strong progress by showing how the amount of money distributed to students had grown in each of the previous five years. However, the meeting also included a testimony from a former recipient, now teaching in the school system, who praised the program that provided for her needs at a time when she did not know where the needed tuition would come from. Attendees walked away with a strong sense of both progress and impact from the program.

Earlier I said that the coincident and temporal patterns would change slightly for each source of input. Balancing the inputs related to purpose involves balancing inside inputs and outside inputs. As all organizations seek to define mission, the agile will also seek to balance supply (inside input) with demand (outside input). As leaders show results for that mission, they must again balance progress (inside output) with impact (outside output).

RESULTS POSTTEST

Please take a moment to revise the list of results indicators that you listed prior to reading this chapter. Refine your statement based upon your learnings and reflections.

RESULTS DISCUSSION QUESTIONS

1. What is one accomplishment in your organization that you are aware of though others may not be?
2. What variable would you like to measure in your organization, but are not sure how to go about it?
3. Are all of your departments aligned with your organizational mission?
4. How do your leaders model execution of strategy?
5. How are results reported in your organization?
6. What do others value from your sphere of influence?
7. What thematic goal might your organization embrace that would potentially involve all of your departments or divisions?
8. What activity might your entire organization embrace that could potentially become a radical leverage point for your future?
9. Name one lag indicator and three lead indicators that may influence it.
10. What is the role of your governing board?

MEASURING RESULTS

For the following list of items, please indicate the extent to which you believe that your organization currently demonstrates these behaviors and activities according to the following schema. As you answer the questions, please draw upon your personal knowledge of your organization during the last six months. Please do not be afraid to use all parts of the spectrum in your responses. Total the responses for your "results" score.

5 = This is true of my organization almost all of the time
4 = This is true of my organization most of the time
3 = This is true of my organization about half the time
2 = This is seldom true of my organization
1 = I cannot recall a time when my organization did this

My organization...

_____ does a great job of reporting to its board of directors and constituents.

_____ proves to others that its priorities are the right priorities.

_____ amazes people with its progress toward its goals.

_____ often uses narrative when reporting on goals.

_____ has measurable goals.

_____ can demonstrate that its adopted goals are the right goals for its focus.

_____ never announces a goal without a strategy and budget to achieve it.

_____ is making a difference in the world.

_____ knows the progress it is making at any particular moment in time.

_____ can point toward specific examples of how this organization has made a difference in the lives of people.

Total the scores for your results total _____.

Total the scores for 1, 3, 5, 7, and 9 _____. This represents your organization's ability to display progress of results.

Total the scores for 2, 4, 6, 8, and 10 _____. This represents your organization's ability to impact others with your missional priorities.

5

Embracing People: *Potential*

Potential——Performance
(strength)   (speed)

Just as every human being has potential, so does every organization because they are also organisms. All organizations have a variety of strengths comprised of the talents, attitudes, and capabilities of their members. How well have you grasped your organization's potential? Strengths can be discovered and they can be developed, but unless others understand them, it is as if they do not exist. Assessing strengths involves discovering people's talents. The most agile organizations are comprised of individuals with complementary skills and talents that add breadth and balance to the organization, allowing it to respond to a wide range of opportunities. For instance, most organizations benefit from someone who can brainstorm possibilities on a "blank page" as well as someone who can successfully implement developed plans. Thus, it may be important to recruit different people who collectively can process all phases of project development. It may also be important to discover how long people have been with the organization, with whom they spend the most time, what energizes the individuals with whom they work, or perhaps what tasks drain them of energy. For the pretest on organizational potential, list below five things that you need to know about your co-workers in order to fully understand your organization's or team's potential.

Potential

Have you ever played bingo? By means of a refresher, every player in the game selects a bingo card containing various numbers. Every card has a different set of numbers, but no one card contains all of the potential numbers that may be called. The caller then begins calling out numbers and the first person to respond with the appropriate sequence wins. Winning sequences vary. Sometimes forming a straight line is required. Other times, filling in the four corners of your card is required. Covering the entire card is another option.

Imagine that the bingo card represents the strengths possessed by people in your organization. Every time that a strength is called out and possessed by one of your members, such as "empathetic listening" or "steady in a crisis," you yell, "Got it!" If no one in your organization possesses that strength, you must remain silent on that particular call. Imagine that the caller is a futurist, who is gauging the environment and calling out strengths required in order to respond effectively to the environmental changes. In this gaming scenario, the first organization yelling, "Bingo!" represents the organization best prepared to respond to that environmental threat or opportunity. How well do you believe that your organization would fare in such a game? Are you are well prepared for some threats, but not others? Would you need to develop a number of strengths in order to yell out, "Got it!" a sufficient number of times? As a leader in your organization, do you possess a sparse card or a full card? If sparse, remember that strengths can be developed as well as discovered.

Understanding the individuals who comprise an organization adds strength to that organization. If you are unaware of any aspect of those strengths it is as if they do not exist. Developing people increases the potential of the organization, but so does discovering gifts. While no source of input can be ignored, an organization will be no greater than the source of its potential as defined by the skills, strengths, and attitudes of its members or employees.

Understanding Personal Gifts

As I alluded to in the introduction, organizations may explore a number of categories in order to assess the strengths and abilities of their members. Below, I list some possibilities.

Preferences

One category of gifts relates to the "built-in preferences" of each member. Preferences show how people are "wired for life." One of the reasons that I especially like these types of assessments is that they reveal gifts, not weaknesses, for every single person. One of my favorites in this category is the Myers-Briggs Type Indicator (MBTI). Chances are that you or at least someone on your team has already taken this instrument. This instrument presents four pairs of gifts and reveals which of each pair the person in your organization possesses, or where along a line between the qualities the person falls:

Breadth OR Depth

Present Enjoyment OR Seeing the Possibilities

Analyzing OR Harmonizing

Organization OR Flexibility

Every person you know will fit somewhere on the line between breadth and depth, for example. No one can possess both completely. On the other hand, everyone will possess some aspect of one or the other, to varying degrees. Speaking of hands, one explanation commonly used for this instrument is that it is like being right-handed or left-handed. You may occasionally use both hands, but clearly one is preferred over the other in most circumstances. This type of instrument can also reveal some of the things that both energize and drain individuals. For instance, the very same activity, such as planning a parade, may energize one and drain another, while the act of leading in the parade may energize someone else.

While the MBTI is widely available for scoring and interpretation, using psychological instruments is not absolutely necessary in order to assess the preferences of people in your organization and in fact should not be used "casually," without the assistance of someone properly trained. Using instruments can greatly enhance the discovery of gifts and potential within an organization, but they should be used in the proper manner.

If you do not have access to a consultant or nearby college or library, or are not skilled at net surfing to discover people trained in the use of psychological instruments, don't wait to access the talents of your members. Simply asking questions such as, "What project did you most enjoy working on during the past year?" "What event did you most appreciate?" "What was your favorite volunteer assignment ever?" "What was the most powerful worship service or event you experienced recently?" "How do you prepare for a big assignment?" or, "How do you get to know others?" can reveal preferences about people. "How" and "what" questions stimulate conversation in this area.

As you discover preferences among members of your organization, make sure to chart them. As with other chapters, you will be asked to rework your pretest at the end of this chapter based upon what you have learned.

Competencies

Skills comprise an important component of organizational potential. Unlike preferences, competencies can be altered or improved, making this a very important assessment category for most organizations. One way to define competencies is "capabilities that could be made stronger." As with preferences, asking questions is a good place to begin assessing competencies. Leaders can begin to assess people's strengths by simply asking them what they are good at: "What are some tasks that come easy for you?" "What skills have others seen in you?" "For what have you received the most recognition in your life?" "Name a skill that you may have taken for granted."

The discussion about competencies can begin by asking probing questions, but it should quickly become much more complex. People may possess hundreds of types of competencies, which fall into many categories. One of the more helpful lists of competencies comes from Howard Gardner, who lists seven areas of *intelligence*, or ways of learning, namely musical, bodily-kinesthetic, logical-mathematical, linguistic, spatial, interpersonal, and intrapersonal.[1] As I suggested in the pretest, it is helpful for organizations to decide what type of information they would like to know about their members. Of Gardner's list, which of those would be important for you to know about your members? Is it important for you to know who is better at building interpersonal relationships or who has strong verbal and communication skills? Does knowing who learns by hearing and who learns by doing help you? What do you need to know about your organization's members to understand your organization's potential?

Competencies are best measured by reliable and validated instruments designed for this purpose. Validity refers to the ability of an instrument to measure what it actually claims to measure. Reliability refers to the ability of the instrument to measure items consistently over time. The instruments I describe in the next few paragraphs have all been shown to be valid and reliable.

One of the most comprehensive instruments for assessing competencies is called *Voices*.[2] Rather than presenting a model of leadership, the authors present a library of competencies because they have demonstrated that different jobs sometimes require nearly opposite competencies. Nearly all competency instruments contain "subscales" or categories of skills. This test measures the subscales of strategy, operating skills, courage, drive, organizational positioning, personal skills, and interpersonal skills. Other examples of competency-based instruments include "Leadership Circle," "Firo-B," and "DISC."

Another popular tool measures *emotional intelligence*. Discovering strengths in the area of emotional intelligence can help you understand how you are contributing to a successful marriage, workplace, or community, as well as reveal why you may be experiencing health problems or unhappiness.[3] These types of measures reveal emotional strengths as opposed to cognitive strengths. The emotional intelligence instrument that I prefer was developed by Reuven Bar-On and contains the subscales of intrapersonal components, interpersonal components, adaptability components, stress management, and general mood.[4]

One of the best means of assessing strengths is through a "360-degree instrument." It seeks feedback from all directions. Typically such instruments will assess the opinions of co-workers, supervisors, friends, family, and colleagues in order to help an individual gain a better understanding of their own strengths. Admittedly, problems have surfaced in administering 360 instruments, generally from misuse. But, when used properly, such instruments can provide much better feedback than self-scored instruments. The ratings of all other people usually correlate better than self-ratings. In my experience, individuals being rated are often eager to share a summary of their newly discovered self with others, including highlighting their most dominant strengths for others to see as well as developing an accountability plan for continued improvement.

Assessing skills and competencies is a key component to understanding organizational potential.

Pathways

In chapter 1, I mentioned archetypes as I discussed how the identity of an organization can be partially formed by the storyline that it is living out. Archetypes can also be helpful for individuals in assessing which pathway or journey they are on and thus can help uncover organizational potential: "People who are interested in human growth and development may understand the archetypes as guides to life's journeys. Each archetype that comes into our lives brings with it a task, a lesson, and ultimately a gift. The archetypes together teach us how to live."[5] Unlike the instrument used to uncover archetypes for organizations, the Pearson-Marr Archetype Indicator is an *unrestricted* instrument, meaning that individuals may purchase the instrument and take it via online or pencil and paper without the assistance of an interpreter.[6] The Pearson-Marr Archetype Indicator reveals which of the following pathways people are currently living out: innocent, orphan, warrior, caregiver, seeker, destroyer, lover, creator, ruler, magician, sage, or jester.

Understanding One Another's Strengths

Encouraging everyone to understand their own preferences, personal strengths, and pathways is only one part of uncovering organizational potential. Agile organizations encourage not only self-discovery of gifts, but also neighbor-to-neighbor discovery of gifts. It is important to know one another's strengths for several reasons.

Why Take the Time?

First, there are simply too many problems and opportunities to be addressed by one person's, or even one unit's, competencies. Understanding the strengths of others makes the difference between simply ignoring an opportunity beyond your particular skill set and capitalizing on the opportunity based upon your awareness of another's strengths.

Second, knowledge of differences can drastically reduce conflicts. In any organization, including the workplace, the church, the service organization, and even families, knowledge of differences reduces conflict. Understanding personal idiosyncrasies is helpful, but such a discovery naturally leads to a more important discovery: that others are wired in a very different manner than oneself. It is this second discovery that prevents me from assuming that others are trying to make life difficult for me. Rather, the more I understand the potential differences in people, the more I understand who they are. It is just as important for individuals to understand why others prefer certain patterns as it is for themselves to understand why they do what they do. Studies have shown that managers invest approximately 40 percent of their time in resolving conflicts among the people who report to them. Understanding one another's differences may reduce that amount.

A third reason to understand one another's strengths is so that people in the organization can serve in the most appropriate positions. Most organizations try to recruit or hire people who are capable of performing the tasks assigned. Agile organizations go beyond that by ensuring that people serve in areas that energize them and build up the organization. Marcus Buckingham reports, "Only twenty percent of employees working in large organizations surveyed feel that their strengths are in play every day. Most bizarre of all, the longer an employee stays with an organization and the higher he climbs the traditional career ladder, the less likely he is to strongly agree that he is playing to his strengths."[7] How about you? Do you feel that your strengths are being utilized every day?

A fourth reason is that understanding differences builds relationships. Indeed, the best way to get to know people is to seek to understand more about their preferences, their abilities, and their passions. It is honoring to be asked what you do well. The goal of every manager should be to empower people to develop competencies beyond the manager's own capabilities. Some avoid this, thinking that it may put their own positions in jeopardy, but it is not true. Someone who can develop and empower others is worth more to an organization than one star performer. Managers threatened by others' strengths never make good managers.

Develop as Well as Discover

As you begin to assess the strengths and competencies possessed by individuals in your organization, you may discover certain deficiencies. For instance, you may discover that no one on your team or in your organization possesses natural visionary skills. Or you may discover a lack of implementation strength. Deficiencies surface from the need to have at least one person in the organization who possesses a given skill. Agile organizations possess a full range of strengths so that they can respond to a full range of opportunities. Deficiencies also come to light when a corporate-wide expectation is not met. If anyone on the team lacks a certain competency that the leader expects everyone to possess—such as the skill of encouraging others, or being a team player, or creativity—then the leader may suggest development work. A consultant can work with your organization to help you discover which skills are tied to performance and results in your field, suggesting how to train and develop the individuals in your organization in areas identified as salient.

Most organizations orient new people into the organization. Agile organizations go beyond that as they offer skill-based workshops for skills that they expect every member to possess and embrace. Agile organizations do not just want everyone to *know* certain things about the organization; they want everyone to be able to *do* certain things. Needed skills emerge from a variety of sources within the organization, such as its stated identity, its preferred vision, its salient mission, or its perceived potential, all of which are covered in this book. Agile organizations value skills equally to knowledge.

Discovering and developing individual strengths always pays off. Berry demonstrates this point in his description of great service organizations:

> Great service companies invest in employees' success. Many firms, tormented by high employee turnover, avoid investing in employees because of their propensity to leave… [T]hese sample companies take the opposite approach. They establish high performance standards for their employees—and equip them to meet the standards successfully… They expect superior achievement and invest in getting it.[8]

Sometimes you have to do the unreasonable to achieve the unexpected. In golf, for instance, I know that if I am slicing and, as a right-handed golfer, I aim to the left to compensate, I will actually worsen my slice. I must turn my body in the direction that I don't want to go in order to hit the ball straight. It is that way with organizations. You must invest in employees, knowing that, in the short run, they may leave, adding to your losses; but, in the long run, it will be a sound investment.

Training and investing in the membership can take an organization to a new level of potential. One of the traditions in a church that I served as pastor was to call a student seminarian as a part-time associate. The person often grew while he or she was in the position, provided very adequate service to the church, and contributed well to the functioning of the church. But in a few years the person would leave and we would look for another. One day I suggested that we invest those same resources in developing the laity of the congregation for a two-year period and then see if we could expand our ministries and resources to the point of being able to call a full-time person to the position with a potentially longer tenure. It worked. We invested in our members by calling in consultants and sending people to national conferences. We purchased equipment and provided tools for ongoing development. In two years the church was able to call a full-time second staff person to the position, who enjoyed a long tenure with the congregation.

Developing Potential with Institutions and Movements

It is important to treat our best assets with care: the valued members of the organization. Because movements exist for outsiders rather than insiders, one of the differences between a movement and an institution is that a movement treats everyone as a customer or as a potential person to serve. In other words, movements take no one for granted, especially those within the organization itself. It is important to treat insiders well because most insiders treat outsiders as they themselves are treated within the organization. This is the golden rule in reverse, and it is as true as the golden rule itself. Members of an organization treat others outside the organization as the organization treats them. Abuse someone and that person will learn to abuse others. Treat someone with respect and that person will model the respect that he or she has been shown.

Treating others within the organization with the highest possible quality of service is paramount, and one of the means of achieving this is to go beyond simply meeting the *needs* of others toward meeting the *expectations* of others. What can make for an even better environment than practicing the golden rule itself is meeting the needs of others, even when they exceed our own needs. Simply applying the golden rule to an organization can lull the members into believing, "If it is good enough for me, than it should be good enough for others." After all, I can satisfy the golden rule simply by treating others the way I want to be treated. Serving others the way Christ served them, however, involves meeting needs that they may have that I do not have. Because a movement is more focused on outsiders than insiders, the members of movements expect outsiders to have different needs than their own, related to services, experiences, development, and support. Movements should serve everyone with distinction, both those inside as well as those outside the organization, by seeking to meet their needs, whatever they may be.

Potential and Balance

In developing people, agile organizations balance the urgency to get people involved with an ability to help them form networks that will enable them to value their sense of involvement. Agile organizations balance participation, involvement, and access with belonging, loyalty, and fit.

Participation is achieved through granting people access to the organization. However, it must be balanced with belonging in order for a person to find a long-term home within an organization. Access does not imply belonging. Many organizations are open and accessible, but do not help people find a sense of belonging. People develop a sense of belonging and loyalty when they find a "fit" within the organization. Simply opening doors or granting people access to the organization cannot achieve fit. It can only be achieved through relationship building between the organization and the individual.

Belonging is a matter of pointing out a match between the interests that a person has and the opportunities within the organization. When a person applies for a job or asks for membership in an organization, the person is announcing that there is a potential match between his or her interests and the activities of that business or organization. Even in a business where people are paid for their participation, leaders have long since discovered that it takes more than a paycheck to truly get people involved in an organization. As organizations take the time to get to know individuals, they can suggest where a person might best serve within the organization.

Participation and belonging are cyclical. Once a person finds a sense of belonging and fit within the organization, leading to an increased sense of loyalty, participation must continue to be encouraged. Even though an individual may come to a sense of belonging through participation, over time involvement may become independent of that sense of belonging. We are all very aware of members of organizations who no longer participate. Sometimes, such members claim great loyalty to the organization, refusing to have their names removed, even though they have not demonstrated that loyalty through participation or involvement in any way for a number of years.

Agile organizations balance participation and belonging by balancing access and fit. Organizations demonstrate access by clearly representing their identity to the world, by developing concise job descriptions for interested employees and clear expectations for their volunteers, and by advertising such opportunities as widely as possible. Organizations enhance fit by offering personality inventories, mentoring programs, and orientation sessions. Both access and fit are enhanced through hosting and networking. Both are essential components of organizational agility.

POTENTIAL POSTTEST

Please take a moment to revise the list of items that you need to know about the members of your organization or team in order to fully understand your organization's potential. Refine your original statement based upon your learnings and reflections. Once you have completed the posttest, you are invited to refer to the sample below.

DEVELOPING ORGANIZATIONAL POTENTIAL

Profile of _____(name)_____MBTI_____

My top three skills/competencies are:

  1.
  2.
  3.

I need an organization that:
(rank from: 1=most needed, to 4=least needed)

_____ Builds a healthy working team and promotes community
_____ Focuses upon demonstrating the results of meeting the needs of customers
_____ Learns new things and consistently innovates the best practices of others
_____ Is stable and secure with clear expectations for all of its employees

The three people in this organization that I spend the most time with are:

1.
2.
3.

I give my best work to a project at the: (*check one*)

_____ Beginning (envisioning stage)

_____ Middle (refinement stage)

_____ End (implementation stage)

My colleagues need to be patient with me when it comes to:

People with the following types of skills complement my work:

People with the following types of characteristics hinder my work:

I am energized when working on projects relating to the following content:

I serve our organization's constituents/customers best when I am:

I usually respond to stress by:

In order for me to buy into a decision, I need the following type of information: *(Check all that apply)*

_____ Knowledge of where and how the idea has been implemented elsewhere

_____ Knowledge of how it will affect our organization's budget and personnel

_____ Knowledge of the greatest possible impact if implemented

POTENTIAL DISCUSSION QUESTIONS

1. List the five most common strengths on your "organizational bingo card."
2. What are the individual preferences of the persons on your team?
3. Ask everyone in your leadership group to state their top three leadership competencies.
4. What competencies best complement your own personal strengths?
5. Name a skill your organization or team needs, but no one possesses.
6. Which storyline are you currently living out: innocent, orphan, warrior, caregiver, seeker, destroyer, lover, creator, ruler, magician, sage, or jester?
7. What percentage of your organization's time is spent handling personality conflicts? How can that be reduced?
8. Name three skills that you believe every member of your organization should possess.
9. What members or employees within your organization are most often taken for granted? What can be done to better serve them?
10. Is your organization better at providing access or fit for people?

MEASURING POTENTIAL

For the following list of items, please indicate the extent to which you believe that your organization currently demonstrates these behaviors and activities according to the following schema. As you answer the questions, please draw upon your personal knowledge of your organization during the last six months. Please do not be afraid to use all parts of the spectrum in your responses. Total the responses for your "potential" score.

> 5 = This is true of my organization almost all of the time
> 4 = This is true of my organization most of the time
> 3 = This is true of my organization about half the time
> 2 = This is seldom true of my organization
> 1 = I cannot recall a time when my organization did this

My organization...

_____ grants people access to all facets of the organization.

_____ arranges people in a way that everyone is doing what they do best.

_____ encourages people to get involved.

_____ provides adequate orientation for new members.

_____ ensures that every member knows where to find whatever they need.

_____ is good at mentoring its members.

_____ constantly seeks new ways of getting people involved.

_____ instills a strong sense of loyalty among its members.

_____ has a lot of people who attend and participate, but do not belong.

_____ has a lot of people who belong, but do not attend or participate.

Total the scores for your potential total _____.

Total the scores for 1, 3, 5, 7, and 9 _____. This represents your organization's ability to get people involved.

Total the scores for 2, 4, 6, 8, and 10 _____. This represents your organization's ability to instill a sense of belonging for individuals within the organization.

6

Embracing People: *Performance*

Potential——Performance
(strength)   (speed)

PERFORMANCE PRETEST

Developing people adds strength to any organization. But for an organization to move, the people must perform. Increased potential should lead to increased performance, but, unfortunately, that is not always the case. Potential and performance are two separate components of an organization and many organizations excel in one and not the other. Enhancing the potential of the organization involves meeting the needs of people in ways that intersect with the skill set needs of the organization. Enhancing the performance of the organization involves discovering ways to encourage, empower, motivate, and inspire activity in the midst of those crossroads between individual needs and organizational needs. Ultimately, each person must contribute to the overall mission and vision of the organization for it to achieve its goals. For the performance pretest, write down, in fifty words or less, how you as an individual are contributing to the advancement of your organization's mission and vision. If you are reading this book in a group setting, ask others to do the same.

Performance

Given the choice of sitting around all day or making a difference in this world, most people would choose to perform. People have an innate desire to perform well. My son had just completed first grade and we were having a chat about the summer. As we talked about how he would like to spend his summer, we talked about summer vacation, friends, games, and trips. I also decided to introduce the concept of "goals." After a very detailed explanation on the treatise of goals with my six-year-old son, he replied, "Sure. I'd like to climb to the top of the big hill, catch a fish in Grandpa's lake, and ride my bike every single day." At the end of the conversation, my daughter, who I was unaware had come into the room, said, "Daddy. I have goals too. I'd like to learn how to ride a bike, read one of Brandon's books, and jump into the deep end of the pool." My daughter had come up with this on her own, without the benefit of my lecture on the concept of goals.

Goals are innate. People want to achieve them in spite of the efforts of their parents and supervisors. Inspiring performance is primarily about ensuring that people are in the right position within the organization, have the tools to do the tasks that they need to do, and are clear about the expectations that the organization has of them. The only piece of performance that does not already come naturally for people is relevance. People naturally want to do well, but they may not be naturally motivated to do well in the ways that the organization wants them to do well. Thus, I begin our discussion about performance with the topic of relevance and then show how we are all naturally gifted to carry out relevant tasks.

Relevance

One of the greatest downfalls of organizations is failing to ensure that each individual is truly contributing to the overall mission and vision of the organization. Every individual contributor to an organization usually assumes that his or her work is relevant to that organization, but unless that relevance can be articulated, that may not be true. One of the best examples of the irrelevance of a group's effort to the overall mission of an organization relates to congregations with evangelism committees, which tend to grow slower than congregations without such committees. The reasons are easily discernable. Normally such committees talk about evangelism more than they practice it. Others in the congregation think that someone else is working on that issue, so they don't. Finally, seldom do the members of an evangelism committee actually have the gift of evangelism themselves. Regardless of how honorable one's work may be, the collective efforts should also advance the mission and vision of the organization.

The best way of ensuring that an individual's efforts are relevant to the mission and vision of the organization is through description. Every person within an organization should not only be able to describe its identity in succinct language, its vision in a brief portrait, and its mission in a concise list, but should also be able to describe how her or his individual efforts are contributing to those pieces. One's relevance may relate directly to making the vision a reality, or it may relate to one or more of the mission priorities, or it may relate indirectly through one or more of the key indicators or lead variables discussed in the chapter on results, but the work must be relevant.

Test this question at your next meeting. Ask participants how each one's individual work is contributing to the overall mission and vision of the organization. For those who struggle with the exercise, announce the date of a future workshop that will address the topic of relevance to the organization and its mission. The key to developing such a workshop will be to translate the mission and vision of the organization into a set of "expectations" for each member. Orientation sessions to the organization should also include this component for new members or employees. In agile organizations, each individual, department, and committee can demonstrate how their personal sets of goals contribute to the overall mission and vision of the organization. Ideally, information from the organization's mission and vision will form the categories for the individuals' performance goals. Ensuring that individual goals are relevant to expected organizational outcomes is a shared task.

Goals

Besides food, water, and shelter, researchers Edward Deci and Richard Ryan have shown that every human has three basic needs: the need for autonomy, the need for competence, and the need for relatedness.[1] No matter what specific goals individuals pursue, they will ultimately pursue goals that enhance their autonomy, competence, and relatedness. If they are forced to do otherwise, they may become ill and eventually cease to perform at all. Thus, it is imperative that individual goals are developed to encourage autonomy, competence, and relatedness. The sections below describe how these three needs can be integrated into the development of individual performance goals.

Self-Generated Goals

People who generate their own sets of goals are more likely to meet those goals. If individuals do not feel that they have a strong sense of input into the formation of their goals, they will rebel against the process. Have you ever said, "No one likes to be told what to do?" It is not only true of you, but it is true of most people that you know. People generally prefer to generate their own set of plans. They prefer to have some sense of control over their future plans. Doing so gives them a sense that they are working toward an even greater sense of autonomy within the organization. Self-generated goals provide a win-win situation. They enhance the autonomy of the individual and increase the ability of that individual to take on more responsibility in the future.

The *Voices* tool that is a part of the "Leadership Architect,"[2] mentioned in the previous chapter, can also help with the development of goals. The instrument contains a list of sixty-seven competencies that have been shown to influence employee performance. By working with someone trained in the use of this instrument, members of the organization "sort cards" in which each competency is listed on one of the cards, in order to develop a set of competencies for the organizational employees as a group or for each specific staff member within the organization. These competencies can then serve as a foundation for the development of an individual's goals.

In every position I have been in, I have provided an annual list of self-generated goals to my supervisor or board at the beginning of the year. Typically, I group the goals into categories, such as administration, building relationships, personal development, consultations, etc. At the end of the year, and at other times in between, I offer a progress report on the results that I have achieved in relation to the goals. In requiring the same of people who directly report to me, over the years I have found that people are nearly always more ambitious than I might have been had I generated their list of goals. Encouraging every individual to design a comprehensive set of goals on an annual basis adds to the agility of the organization by adding speed and movement to the organization.

In agile organizations, all members perform their own unique roles every year. The alternative is to develop long-term performance standards or evaluate performance against a constant job description. Such inflexibility in the standards or the job description, however, can rapidly lead to stagnation within the organization. Ideally, every person's goals will change each year according to each person's own level of development and according to the maturing mission of the organization. Another alternative in responding to the environment is to develop a two-or-three-year goal set that demonstrates how the individual will develop new skills and respond to new opportunities as the organization matures.

Obviously, there are exceptions to this perfect world of self-generated goals. At this point, you may be thinking, "Sometimes circumstances arise that affect people's performance and these circumstances must be addressed. Surely, the notion of self-generation ceases at this point, right? If they are not able to follow their initial list of their own goals, the supervisor must intervene and provide the individual with a 'corrected list' of goals, right?" Wrong. Self-generated adjustments are even more important to one's performance than self-generated goals.

Self-Generated Adjustments

Recall the reasons for encouraging self-generated goals rather than handing a list of goals to a volunteer or staff person. Self-generated goals enhance the person's sense of autonomy within the process and build ownership over the goals. At that point, these goals are no longer the organization's goals, but rather they are internalized within the individual's identity, life, and personality. Given the opportunity, individuals will design goals that play to their strengths, maximize the tasks that energize them, and build in compensators for less well developed skills. All of these qualities are even more paramount when a person is experiencing a set of difficult circumstances that are affecting performance. In the midst of crisis, the individual needs to feel that he or she still has some sense of control over life's circumstances. Removing the control that was once present in the production of the individual's own goals will only exacerbate the person's downward spiral. Keeping the individual involved in the reformation of the goals is vital to the person's health and long-term performance within the organization. It is the right thing to do even if not the common thing to do, as Rod Napier and Rich McDaniel suggest: "This conscious refinement of definitions and alignment of expectations is the very foundation of employee relationship management, but it is clearly not common practice."[3]

Another benefit of self-generated adjustments is the removal of the excuses that may arise in the future. At the moment that a performance adjustment is being forced upon someone, that individual is probably generating excuses about why the solution will not work. Remember: autonomy is natural; submission is not. If people are given the opportunity to design their own detours, they will again design ones that best fit their personalities and ones that capitalize upon their strengths. If they are actively involved in the discussion, they have no time to generate excuses in their heads.

So, just how might this conversation take place? Imagine that you have noticed a change in the performance in one of your staff members. The first step that you should take as a supervisor is to document the change as accurately as you can. Do not say, "Bill, I have noticed that your attitude is not the same that it was a month ago." Rather, choose some evidence that cannot be refuted. The best evidence is an event that has gone awry, something that Bill had planned for that did not go according to plan, or perhaps even an altercation, or a conflict. The goal of the initial few moments of the conversation is to help Bill name the shift that has taken place and own the change in results. Most individuals are very aware of the changes that have taken place and often the shift may have been occurring long before the supervisor noticed. On the other hand, individuals who lack self-awareness tend to have greater difficulty adjusting their performance efforts. The most productive means of helping individuals who lack self-awareness is to encourage them to work with a coach or mentor, preferably one who has the ability to interpret 360–degree feedback.

Acknowledgement of the change in behavior should be done in such a way that the person sees the lacuna between the expectations of the organization and his or her own performance behavior. The gap may be between the person's performance and the goals that he or she has set, or between behavior and policy, or between the performance of peers and the performance of the individual. The more abstract the goals of the organization, the more difficult this reality check will be to bring about. The second step is to ask, "How do you think this gap can be bridged?" If the person has truly acknowledged the gap for him- or herself, the role of the supervisor or coach will be to help the individual design a reasonable plan for improvement. Redesigned goals should be even more specific than the original set, as well as shorter in length and briefer in scope. Often, the employee is so thankful for a second chance that they will be more ambitious than they need to be in the revisions. Make sure that the goal raises the bar of performance beyond their most recent level of performance, but help the person design a *reasonable* adjustment plan.

Obviously, one possibility is that the person may come to the conclusion that he or she is just not suited for the position that he or she is in. When such an understanding comes to the surface, the organization should help the person relocate to another department within the organization or to another organization. Obviously, there are those rare instances when an employee is incapable of performing in a certain role and does not realize it. In my experience, it is more a matter of the person refusing to realize it rather than being incapable of realizing it. By pointing out the expectations of the role and giving a person several unsuccessful opportunities, a supervisor can generally lead most persons to come to their own conclusion that a certain role is not a good fit for them.

Employees and Volunteers

It makes no difference whether or not a person is an employee or a volunteer within an organization in terms of performance issues. Volunteers can create goals and will benefit from them just as much as employees. An increasing number of volunteers are seeking experiences that truly make a difference in the organization, often in a role that the organization assumed could only be performed by a paid employee. As more Baby Boomers semi-retire with fewer daily obligations, they look for meaningful volunteer experiences. Such experiences should also include evaluation. Everyone appreciates feedback, even volunteers. Feedback should always include areas of celebration as well as areas of potential development, and volunteers need both.

If a person is not performing well, regardless of whether the person is an employee or a volunteer, the situation must be addressed. Persons in poor performance situations are never happy and will only become more miserable the longer that they stay in those roles. Persons performing poorly should be reminded of the expectations of their roles regardless of whether or not they are being paid to perform those roles. In time, even volunteers will usually come to the conclusion that they are not fitted for certain roles after a few well-intentioned attempts have failed to meet the desired expectations.

Different Standards for Institutions and Movements

In addition to individually tailored goals, you might consider developing universal goals for your organization or team. Such goals are common in many organizations and may exist in the form of sales goals or customer satisfaction standards in the business sector. This is also a place, however, where institutions will differ from movements. The standards for institutions seldom change. Higher education admissions offices and military branches ask each recruitment officer to recruit a certain number of persons every year to the organization. Surgeons of hospitals are expected to perform a certain number of surgeries every year. Account representatives are expected to maintain standard client lists.

Movements, however, take this concept to another level by developing universal performance standards that help the organization leap toward its destination rather than merely maintain the quality of the institution. For instance, imagine that you are a member of a congregation focused upon congregational transformation. In helping an organization transform from one identity to another, research has shown that the more people there are within that organization who possess skills of dealing with ambiguity, or understanding multiple perspectives, or performing creatively, the better chance the organization will have of actually transforming. Thus, the congregation might ask each member to attend a workshop or training event where those skills are taught. In addition to whatever individual or departmental goals the church may encourage, the congregation might also encourage all members to enhance their sense of creativity for the coming year. A school with a vision of interacting better with the families of its students might ask every teacher and employee to commit to enhance their listening and compassion skills and hold in-service workshops for the development of those competencies. The employees of a nonprofit focused upon becoming more efficient might commit to enhancing their current level of performance related to time management and priority setting.

What if a physicians group desiring to become more patient friendly focused on the skill of being more patient? Further imagine that the members of a physicians group rewarded those who spent the longest amount of time with their patients rather than the least. Research shows that most physicians interrupt a patient within eighteen seconds after they start talking. One physician asserts, "The errors that we make in our thinking often come about because we cut off the dialogue."[4] Group goals can radically alter performance and can have life-changing results. Workers at Kimley-Horn and Associates reward themselves for all phases of performance. They can actually reward each other with a bonus of $50.00 for outstanding performance. "At any time, for any reason, without permission, any employee can award a bonus of that amount to any other employee.

No strings."[5] Movements develop a set of performance standards common to every person by asking the questions, "What will it take for our organization to achieve our vision?" "What skills must we develop?" "What competencies count the most in the advancement of our mission?"

Effort

Once goals have been established, efforts toward those goals must be celebrated and encouraged by the organization.

Challenge and Support

Encouraging effort involves maintaining a balance between challenge and support. Recall that every human being has a built-in desire to develop competencies. The primary reason for individuals leaving an organization and joining another is a lack of development and growth opportunities. Most organizations err on the side of too little challenge rather than too much. Employees and volunteers must be consistently challenged to move beyond their current competency levels in order to stay energized. In challenging someone to move beyond a current skill that he or she has, the person should still be given a sense of autonomy even with the new task. Just because someone has not performed a task before does not mean that the individual may not have a better way of accomplishing it than the person prior, or at least a method more suited to that person's own set of strengths and gifts.

Such a challenge, however, must be balanced with an appropriate level of support. Remember that balance, along with speed and strength, is one of the three essential components of agility. Picture a person sitting in the middle of a balanced teeter-totter. One side of the teeter-totter is labeled "challenge" and the other "support." Life could get quite boring sitting in that balance day after day. In order to make life more interesting, pressure is placed on the challenge end of the fulcrum or spectrum. But, in order to bring the teeter-totter back into balance, more support must also be given. It will be up to the individual to find an equilibrium point between the challenge presented and the support offered, but both must be made available lest the person crash to the ground.

Evaluation

Once every person has generated a list of goals, assessment is merely a matter of assessing progress on each person's personal goals. Were the goals met? Why or why not? What can enhance the future meeting of those goals? Which goals should be abandoned totally and what areas might be added? At their best, performance evaluations involve a two-way process of discovering what the individual can do to greater enhance the individual's contribution to the overall mission and vision of the organization as well as what the organization can do to enhance the performance of the individual. Napier suggests, "Performance reviews can be dialogues, two-way assessments deliberately designed to evaluate and improve the exchange of value between individuals and the company."[6]

I also recommend the inclusion of a sheet entitled, "Performance response to opportunities that could not be foreseen at the beginning of the year." It is impossible to foresee every opportunity that may arise for the organization to live out its mission and vision in new ways, especially for agile organizations. Thus, every member of the organization should be given the opportunity and indeed be encouraged to respond to opportunities that arise during the year. Many agile organizations build in a certain percentage of time, such as 5–15 percent, for their staff to respond to opportunities in the environment. Such environmental responses may mean that the individual may not have been able to meet some of the other *a priori* goals established at the beginning of the calendar year, but such a decision should be a part of the annual assessment.

Development

Even though performance evaluations are necessary in order to ensure that an individual is contributing to the advancement of the organization's mission and vision, the greater emphasis in such assessment should be placed upon development rather than assessment. If individuals are encouraged to develop or enhance competencies that are directly related to the organization's mission and vision, then such development will ensure performance and such relevance will ensure that organizational indicators are met. If employees develop new competencies every year, they will usually perform well and, as discussed earlier, have a greater chance of staying with the organization.

Satisfaction

Studies have shown that an employee's satisfaction level is highly correlated with turnover and tenure within the organization. Additionally, studies have shown that it is the intrinsic nature of the job that most leads to employee satisfaction. A recent study from the *Pulpit and Pew Project* confirmed that it is the intrinsic factors that most satisfy pastors of local churches, factors such as congregational morale, feeling loved and cared for by the congregation, and tackling new challenges together. My experience tells me that it is the same with regional or judicatory staff, the people with whom I work with the most. They are most satisfied in their roles when making a difference in congregational renewal, clergy development, and meeting needs beyond the reach of any single congregation.

Whenever an organization takes strides to aid the satisfaction of their employees or members, such strides will always be rewarded. Satisfied members work smarter and stay longer with the organization. Organizations desiring to enhance employee satisfaction should concentrate on helping their members feel a part of something visionary and worthwhile, showing appreciation for work well done, hiring caring and competent supervision, involving everyone in decisions that affect the team, providing fair compensation as well as opportunities for professional development, offering feedback on performance, promoting honest communication, and, finally, offering a fun work environment.

Teamwork

Remember that individuals have a built-in need to perform well in ways that enhance further autonomy and performance. Individuals also have a built-in need to relate to other people. That is good news, because individuals are not the only ones who respond to opportunities, tasks, and projects; teams also respond.

Calling a group of people a team will not make them a team. "No corporate mandate or newly hatched initiative can guarantee that the promise of high performance will become anything more than another T-shirt logo or phrase in a long list of meaningless verbiage."[7] Teams are formed not by language, but rather by spending time together working on tasks that contribute to the organization's mission and vision. Covering the same topics with a set of individuals is not team-building. Team building can only occur as people interact with each other in groups. Agile organizations not only add speed to the organization by tracking performance, they place performance in a group loop, which ultimately enables all members of the team to go beyond their original expectations.

Definition of a Team

Even though teamwork can magnify the performance of individuals, developing teams is not an easy process. The word *team* comes from *deuk*, meaning to "pull." It is just as common for teams to pull against each other as it is for them to pull with each other as they try on, discard, and develop each individual's role that will best contribute to the functioning of the group as a team. Ultimately, the only way for teams to truly work together is to have something else outside of the team pulling on them. That "other thing" can be a goal, a leverage point, or an ambition, but it is the key to developing teams. Teams respond best to an issue of importance larger than any of the individual interests contained in the group.

Many groups simply change the name "department" to "team," but a well-functioning team requires more than merely a name change. A group of individuals working side by side is not a team. Personally, I like Gregory Huszczo's definition: "A team requires the interactive use of the skills of the small group of people working together in an interdependent manner to accomplish common goals."[8] Teamwork implies cooperation, and true cooperation leads to synergy. Synergy results when the team accomplishes more than the aggregate potentials of the individuals. As teams interact, they encourage and challenge one another, they refine one another's work, they raise questions that no one person would have asked, and they produce products beyond the imaginations of the individuals. Reaching such a level of team development takes time. Fortunately, in achieving such a product, teams have an identifiable pattern of development from which we can learn as we promote team development.

Stages of Team Development

The development of a team follows a fairly predictable pattern. Teams must develop in stages and the stages often take time. Chances are that you might have heard of the stages of "Forming, Storming, Norming, and Performing." While similar, I prefer Susan Wheelan's language of (1) Dependency and Inclusion, (2) Counter-Dependence and Fight, (3) Trust and Structure, and (4) Work and Productivity.[9]

The important point is not the precise labels of development, but rather capturing the concept that developing teams requires time and progresses through a set of stages. Whenever I consult with teams I ask the members to assess their current stage of development and then work with them to set a goal and a timetable for where they would like for their team to be in the future. Typically, the designated leader of the team assesses the group as being far ahead of where it is discerned to be by the others. Leaders underestimate the work, energy, conflict, and time required for team development. The rewards of team development are worth it, but the beginning costs are real and often underestimated by team leaders.

No team can begin working as a high performance team on the first day. "Teams must take the time necessary to know one another, build camaraderie, and understand each member's passion, gifts, and spiritual journey."[10] As the team is negotiating roles, jockeying for position, and establishing boundaries during the middle stages of team development, the team will probably produce less than the collective potential of the individual members. It is at this place that many teams abandon the group process. The problem is that they usually abandon the team at the moment where the greatest strides lie just ahead.

Team Relationships

One of the best ways of building teams is to start with people who like working with others, typically known as "team players." Certain individuals are either not predisposed to working on a team or have developed a sufficient number of bad habits as to make them poor team players. It is unrealistic to expect those individuals to develop into team players merely by placing them on a team. Individual intervention may be required to help them understand their deficiencies in this area prior to expecting them to function well on a team.

Once a dysfunctional team member gets on a team, the misbehavior must be addressed: "If people who get involved are awkward with one another, you have four options: coach them on the appropriate style, replace them with others, reduce your expectations, or end the discussions."[11] The true potential of any team will be measured by the development of the relationships on the team.

The Purpose of Teams

While individuals have an innate need for relatedness, organizational teams develop for a purpose that extends beyond the social needs of their members. The most common activity of teams is problem solving. In his "action-learning" model, Marquardt suggests a four-step process for teams tackling problems.[12]

Stage 1: Understanding and reframing the problem
Stage 2: Framing and formulating the goal
Stage 3: Developing and testing strategies
Stage 4: Taking action and reflecting on the action

The highest performing teams are learning teams. Thus, Marquardt suggests incorporating an action learning coach into team process. Try this the next time that your team takes on a new assignment or task. Designate someone on the team as the team learner or, better yet, bring someone in specifically to play the role of an observer and feedback giver. I have been a part of several teams with a built-in observer and have always benefited from the experience. If played by a member of the group, the role may be rotated, but the idea is to empower someone to ask tough questions, help the group reflect, and enable the group to become a learning community.[13] One of the benefits of action learning is that the questioning process always causes the participants to become more interested in the problem.

Another key to team functioning is the productivity of the team meetings. The following parameters can help:

- Announce how each meeting will contribute to the overall team or organizational goals
- Develop agendas in advance with the input of each team member
- Stick to the agenda during meetings
- Brainstorm something at every meeting
- Have no more than three discussion/action items in one meeting
- Celebrate your progress at the end of each meeting

Patrick McKenna makes the following additional suggestions to aid team performance:[14]

- Ask the members of your group to articulate what's in it for them
- Give everyone the opportunity to stand up and declare his or her personal commitment
- Focus first on what you can do now, with existing resources
- Encourage experimentation
- Build for an early success to continue the momentum
- Search continually for opportunities for people to create or outdo themselves
- Focus on the excitement of the endeavor

Competing Teams

Some organizations ask teams to compete with one another. The greatest difficulty in this practice lies in ensuring a level playing field for all teams involved. But, if that can be ensured, friendly competition always enhances performance, especially among teams. Congregations have asked Sunday school classes or other small groups to compete in attendance or learning goals, school classrooms have competed in donations for a community cause, and service organizations have competed with one another in community fundraising. In tracking performance, it is also wise to ask teams to get involved in tracking one another's performance by "making shared measurement the foundation of joint management."[15]

Performance and Balance

As leaders guide people from incubation to journey, they move from developing potential to inspiring performance. In enhancing member performance, agile organizations balance accountability and empowerment. Accountability is a coincident pattern, while empowerment is a temporal pattern. For prime organizational performance, the two patterns should be balanced within the organization. Many organizations overemphasize one or the other, which is a prescription for major organizational problems. Agile organizations balance the tracking of employee performance with the development of the employee's competencies.

Organizations that overemphasize accountability stifle employee creativity. Some employees spend so much time generating reports that they have no time left over for generating ideas or creating value among their clients and customers. Some of the best ideas surface apart from any policy or procedure put in place by a manager. Agile leaders empower their employees, their subordinates, their volunteers, and their members through encouragement, motivation, and coaching. An empowered worker is creative, competent, and inspired. Empowering workers is also the key to building job satisfaction and job performance within the organization.

With no accountability, even the most motivated person in the world could be performing activities completely outside of the organization's defined mission. Members or employees must also be held accountable for their activities. Even volunteers want to be held accountable. They want to know that the tasks they are doing are not only appreciated, but are also needed by the organization. Accountability conversations and even behavioral modification plans can still be self-generated as discussed earlier, but they do need to occur. Organizations that lack accountability give rise to unfair employee practices and often create dissatisfaction among their most prized members. Stars will not perform long in an environment that closes its eye toward others who slack. Organizations must ensure that members contribute to the mission and vision to the best of their ability. Agile organizations balance the autonomy of the individual with an interdependence upon others.

PERFORMANCE POSTTEST

Based upon your learnings and reflections from this chapter, please take a moment to revise your performance pretest by writing down how you as an individual are contributing to the advancement of your organization's mission and vision

PERFORMANCE DISCUSSION QUESTIONS

1. Who are the best performing individuals that your organization has ever had? What made them so?
2. How do you deal with people who are poor performers?
3. Could your organization initiate the $50.00 reward? If not, could another reward item be substituted to make the implementation possible?
4. What unusual universal standard could your organization implement for all of its members?
5. How well do the members of your organization listen to one another? How many seconds do your members average in listening to one another before cutting one another off?
6. Think about all of the teams or committees within your organization or department. What is the purpose of each? How is each member contributing to those purposes?
7. In what stage is the team in which you work?
8. What are some of your own best practices that make for productive team meetings?
9. Is your organization better at offering challenge or support?
10. Is your organization better at empowerment or accountability?

MEASURING PERFORMANCE

For the following list of items, please indicate the extent to which you believe that your organization currently demonstrates these behaviors and activities according to the following schema. As you answer the questions, please draw upon your personal knowledge of your organization during the last six months. Please do not be afraid to use all parts of the spectrum in your responses. Total the responses for your "performance" score.

5 = This is true of my organization almost all of the time
4 = This is true of my organization most of the time
3 = This is true of my organization about half the time
2 = This is seldom true of my organization
1 = I cannot recall a time when my organization did this

My organization...

_____ believes that individuals know how to contribute best to the organization.

_____ has clear standards for accountability.

_____ gives people great leeway to go about their identified tasks.

_____ expects people to perform at their highest level.

_____ empowers its members to make a difference.

_____ has a well-designed performance appraisal system.

_____ shows much appreciation to its members.

_____ follows up with people to ensure performance.

_____ supplies adequate resources and technology to its members to allow them to work at peak performance.

_____ holds its members accountable to one another for group performance.

Total the scores for your performance total _____.

Total the scores for 1, 3, 5, 7, and 9 _____. This represents your organization's ability to empower people.

Total the scores for 2, 4, 6, 8, and 10 _____. This represents your organization's ability to hold people accountable.

7

Embracing Assets: *Capacity*

Capacity——Allocations
(strength)   (speed)

CAPACITY PRETEST

How financially constrained is your organization? Is your organization operating out of a sense of fear for its financial future or out of a sense of trust that your mission and your efforts to support it will allow your organization to produce the kind of results promised? Are the other components of your organization working to enhance or limit your fundraising efforts? This chapter will explore the rubric of building the capacity of your organization through fundraising and the components that affect it. For this chapter's pretest, please rank the following groups of givers to your organization in terms of how well your organization is doing connecting with each type of giver. The categories are not meant to be mutually exclusive, meaning that some givers may fall into more than one category. Please rank the categories from 1 to 5, giving a "1" to the group that you are best connected with and a "5" to the group to which you are least connected. When you finish your rankings, each group should have been assigned a different number.

_____ Insiders
_____ Inclined
_____ Investors
_____ Invited
_____ Indebted

Capacity

All organizations need money to operate. Businesses need money to pay their employees and shareholders. Nonprofits need money to fund their staff and their mission. Congregations need money to make a difference in their communities as well as globally. Few organizations can function without funds.

Organizations can be either strengthened or weakened by their financial holdings. Increasing assets can greatly strengthen an organization. Even though it may not be written down, nearly all organizations have a "must list" as well as a "wish list" of projects that they would pursue if only the money allowed for such. Many organizations are short on finances, but organizations are never short on dreams. Funding dreams merely leads to dreaming more dreams. Imagination may be the stuff that dreams are made of, but money is what makes them a reality. Building capacity adds strength, and increased strength, in turn, adds to the organization's potential. As organizations begin to tackle some of their wish list items in addition to their "paying the dues" activities, the organizations gain momentum, allowing for more new projects to be funded. Funding wish lists also expands the range of donors as varying types of projects lead to varying types of donations. Only a limited number of people will significantly fund the annual budget of an organization. Many others, however, will fund the organization's special projects, dream ventures, and wish lists. Tapping into different sources of funding can add tremendous strength to an organization. Failing to do so will cause an organization to be limited by the giving of its insiders, which can cause the organization to become anemic over time.

Short-Term and Long-Term Capacity

Just like households, organizations need to build both short- and long-term capacity. Just as individuals can get into trouble by living "paycheck to paycheck," so can organizations. The rule of thumb for individuals is to have at least six months wages in the bank for an emergency situation. That figure should be at least doubled for organizations. I am amazed at how many organizations have only one or two months of income set aside for emergencies, or, as occurs more frequently, set aside to cover the shortfall while a new funding strategy is adopted. It is a myth to think that nonprofits are any less vulnerable than businesses when it comes to income. Businesses depend upon customer loyalty and nonprofits depend upon member loyalty. Thus, both need some funds set aside for the long term in order to respond to shifts in constituent loyalty.

On the other hand, some organizations have plenty of security for the long term, but very little funds to operate on a daily basis. Some organizations have large sums that are restricted to certain missional objectives, or have a huge portion of their assets tied up in endowments that do not allow for short-term usage. Other organizations have all of their money tied up in buildings and grounds and very little available for programming or carrying out their mission. Organizations need both short-term cash flow as well as long-term funding capacity.

The methods listed below will help an organization increase its capacity, but first a word about attitude.

Organizational Attitude

Throughout this book, I have lifted up the importance of intangibles and encouraged the reader to treat them equally to the more tangible aspects of organizational life. Surely, when we get to the chapter on assets, tangibles trump intangibles, right? After all, money talks. Wrong. Money may talk, but attitude walks. Lingering deficiencies in brand image, employee outlook, departmental conflict, leadership viewpoint, and overall morale can greatly affect an organization's ability to raise dollars, as can its attitude toward dollars in general.

Organizations need endowments, cash flow, credit lines, and solid commitments from potential donors. And, the attitude that an organization has toward assets can radically affect its ability to garner them. Does your organization operate out of an "abundance posture" or a "scarcity posture"? Do the members of your organization concentrate more on money than mission? Are your agendas consumed by discussions about how to manage the money that you have or how to increase the capacity of your organization? Jim Collins and others have shown that concentrating on money as the bottom line is not a healthy long-term strategy.[1] Organizations operating out of an abundance mindset do not focus upon survival; instead, they focus upon the mission of the organization and simply present opportunities to fund it. Organizations operating out of a scarcity mindset are so concerned about the possible death of the organization that they focus all of their energies upon their continued existence. Have you heard the phrase, "No one wants to give to a sinking ship"? It is true. No one wants to fund the Titanic. They may want to purchase the antiques and artifacts before they end up at the bottom of the ocean, but they do not want to pay anyone's way aboard, especially their own. This is one of those anomalies in organizational life. The more an organization focuses upon survival, they less likely it is to survive.

Building Capacity within Institutions and Movements

Focusing fundraising efforts on survival rather than mission is a much greater temptation for institutions than movements. With respect to capacity, the major difference between movements and institutions is that movements fund mission, while institutions fund the components to make the mission happen. It is a subtle difference, but an important one. Institutions encourage donors to fund the ongoing existence of the institution in order to have an infrastructure in place to mold and empower the mission. Movements always encourage their donors to directly fund mission, causes, and concerns. Obviously, organizations need to attract donors who are interested in funding the institutional part as well as donors interested in funding the missional part of their organization.

Attracting donors is the subject we turn to next as we take a look at why people give. Agile organizations find a way to appeal to all five of the groups listed in the following section in order to strengthen their organization.

Individual Motivations

This section details the motivations of five different types of donors. Just as agile organizations focus upon multiple outcomes with multiple layers of leaders, they also find a way to appeal to a multiplicity of donors.

Insiders

In every organization, some people consider themselves "insiders." They are "in the know," "in the mainstream," and "in the heart of things." Insiders feel a genuine need to contribute to the capacity of the organization in order to keep it moving because of their connection to it. They feel a responsibility to increase the organization's capacity at all levels, and thus will usually contribute at every level: the annual budget, special projects, long-term building and program funds, and overall endowment. Plus, they have probably already included the organization in their will and may not feel the need to inform the leaders of such an action. To an insider, bequests are simply the right thing to do and need no advertisement. Stories abound of individuals who leave a sizable portion of their estate to organizations whose leaders are unaware of their commitment or ability to give at such levels.

One way to discover insiders is to take a look at those who already volunteer for your organization. This is especially true of congregations. George Barna states, "My research also confirmed a powerful link between giving money and giving time to a church. In short, the best donors are the church's volunteers. Volunteers are the people who have the highest stake in the church's ministry."[2] Insiders are connected. They volunteer. They respond to phone calls. They ask the right questions. They care about your organization's future. All organizations have insiders. Agile organizations appeal to their insiders in such a way that they are able to fund the majority of their infrastructure through insider giving alone.

Insiders contribute from a sense of supporting the community to which they belong. This is true of every culture, but especially the Latino and Asian cultures. According to Michael Cortes, the reason for the increase of Latino nonprofit organizations has been the emphasis upon "defending and renewing the community of identities of Latinos and creating a greater sense of solidarity among Latinos"[3] Stella Shao points out that, as in the Latino culture:

> The Asian American culture of giving can, thus, be seen as an integral part of everyday life. It is based on commonly held beliefs in the value of compassion, the importance of relationships with families and communities, and in the reciprocity of gift-giving and relating, ceremonially, and ritualistically carried out at each occasion throughout life. Philanthropy is not considered a separate categorical concept. Asians give because of their understanding that benevolence, compassion, interdependence, and basic respect for humankind are necessary ingredients to living, first in their families, then in their own communities, and then in the greater society.[4]

Insiders give because they feel that they are an integral part of the communal aspect of the organization. There is no "us" and "them" for insiders; there is only a "we." Thus, organizations can appeal to the propensity of their insiders to give by emphasizing the sense of community within the organization. Appeals can be crafted as a responsibility of the whole. Organizations can also appeal to their insiders by providing them with inside information. Insiders generally want copies of the organization's detailed budget, annual report, departmental outcomes, and future goals. Because they helped build the organization's mission and vision, they feel obligated to fund it. In one organization that I led, I produced an insider's newsletter. The primary difference between the insider's newsletter and the news that went to the wider audience was timing. The insiders received the same information, but they received it sooner than everyone else. I made the timing of the information clear to them and invited them to respond prior to the wider dissemination of the information. I would often receive helpful comments on how to word the news in a more dramatic or appealing fashion for the wider constituency. The insider's newsletter was a "win" for all involved.

Because insiders consider themselves to be an integral part of the organization to which they belong, there is also a group loyalty or even "peer pressure" factor to their giving. One insider may compel another insider to "step up to the plate" and give at an appropriate level of support. Or a group of insiders may meet on their own, without any prompting from the organization's staff, and strategize about how to meet a financial need. This is especially true of Christian organizations. James Hudnut-Buemler writes, "The most important thing to emerge from insight into the ebb and flow of 'Christian' ways to raise money is that unified approaches to religious finance are highly dependent upon social consensus."[5]

Insiders are not only emotionally connected to the organization; they are also emotionally and socially connected to one another. Such connections present unique opportunities to appeal to this group in ways that are not possible with any other group listed below. Because of this group's extreme loyalty, more creative means can be employed with this group than any other. This group can serve equally well as a focus group, as a brainstorming group, and as an implementation group to assist fundraising efforts. If a mistake is made in the marketing appeal of a particular project, insiders will usually be quite forgiving. Ironically, the appeals made to this group are often the most repetitive of any group, with the same words, approach, and tactics duplicated year after year. This is truly a shame, given that the organization's greatest potential for increased capacity lies with its insiders.

Inclined

The second source of potential donors is also a type of insider. These individuals, however, do not consider themselves insiders to a particular organization, but rather they consider themselves insiders to a particular cause. Thus, I term this group the "inclined." They are already inclined to give if their favorite cause is highlighted before them. Those who may not be connected well enough to a particular organization to consider themselves insiders may still have a propensity to give if their favorite cause is lifted up before them. We live in a special interest society. People are already attached to causes and are simply looking for ways to fund them. Hudnut-Buemler supports this notion and writes, "Rapid social change is probably the source of the proliferation of new charities making direct appeals since 1980 based on concern for homelessness, AIDS, international globalization, and increasing income disparity."[6] The number of causes seems to be growing every day.

The way to appeal to the inclined is to lift up particular causes that your organization already addresses or is in a unique position to address because of your personnel and membership mix. If you are a sodality (defined in the mission chapter), then this will be easy; simply highlight your primary reason for existence in places where people gather to support that cause. Attend trade shows, offer to lead workshops at conferences, network with others directly and tangentially related to your cause. If you are a modality, then you might consider highlighting different causes at different times. You may consider highlighting a different cause every year that you support through your mission involvement. Or you might consider promoting direct involvement in one of your missional emphases on an annual basis. Other organizations may choose to emphasize a particular cause for a decade. For example, a national missional agency is currently highlighting "children in poverty," and the denomination's international missional agency is combating "human trafficking." While each agency has a number of other causes they are addressing, they are giving more visible attention to these causes and appealing to those inclined to give or get involved in such a cause.

Investors

> People who earn relatively large sums of money or who have more disposable wealth have generally reached that place in life because of their unique understanding and perspectives related to money and wealth. Communicating effectively with them often requires that they be approached differently and handled differently.[7]

Often, people of wealth consider their giving as an investment, although this mindset is not limited to this constituency.

People generally invest in an organization in order to get something in return. The most common form of donation investing is from those seeking to make an impact with their giving. Unlike those inclined to give to a particular cause, investors can be persuaded to give to something that may be outside of their primary area of interest if it can be shown that their donation will produce a good return on their investment through a substantial impact. Appealing to this type of donor requires more than mere networking. Investors want to see results. They want to hear stories of how their dollars have influenced others in a positive way. They want to hear how their dollars have served as a catalyst for others to give to the same cause. Investors are looking for leverage through their monetary donation. They want to hear how their dollars have opened up new avenues of missional activity not previously available to this organization. Ideally, they want to create a missional impact that no other organization has been able to achieve.

Searching for impact is not the only type of return that investor donors pursue. Other types of investors search for a more personal form of reciprocity through their giving. Some may view their investment as a means of getting more connected to the organization to which they donated. They may desire to become an insider and seek to accomplish that through their donation. Thus, investors should always be given appropriate means of getting more involved. Obviously, some investors may be out to micromanage the organization or control a specific area.

Other investors may view their monetary investment as a return for services rendered by the organization. Members of a church may invest in the congregation with the expectation that pastoral care will be provided for their family members when needed, that someone will be available to preach their funeral, or in appreciation for the opportunities to worship and learn with others. Often such motivations are not conscious, but the investment comes with a certain expectation that the donor will receive something of worth from the donation.

One form of potential investment specific to congregations and religious institutions may be from an individual seeking something in return from God. While congregations and institutions abound who promote this form of giving, sometimes termed "health and wealth gospel preaching," I caution those who become involved in this approach to make sure that the ethics of such a promotion are consistent with the values of the organization itself. As we will see in the next chapter, consistency is also something that must be maintained in the allocation and distribution of funds.

Indebted

Many individuals give because they feel indebted to a particular organization. Often, people may choose to give to an organization because the organization has provided a significant service to them. Those who give out of a sense of indebtedness are not expecting anything in return; they give out of a sense of gratitude. A member of a congregation may give to a local church out of an extreme sense of thankfulness for what God, the church staff, and the members have done for him or her over the years. An individual may choose to give to the local hospice chapter in gratitude for the care received for a terminally ill family member. Parents of a college student may give out of gratitude for the ways that their son or daughter grew during those college years. People often choose to give because they are grateful for what the organization has done for them, expecting nothing more in the future. Those indebted to an organization often feel that they can never repay what has already been received. Jean Fairfax further explains this form of indebtedness giving:

> The concept of "giving back" has always differed, I believe, from that of "reciprocity," which is a deeply honored value that has produced historic and often elaborate rituals in many cultures. In reciprocity there is usually the expectation of a mutual or equivalent exchange among persons who know each other or have some kind of relationship. But giving back is an outpouring of gratitude for what has been received (and it may not be a material benefit), often from unknown benefactors.[8]

Obviously, gratitude giving is the most difficult form of giving for an organization to cultivate, but it can be done through superior service, radical commitment to organizational goals, and incredible customer care.

Invited

The most common mistake that organizations make in fundraising is that they forget to ask for funds to support their mission. Many organizations do an exceptional job of highlighting their mission, but fail to tell those interested how to support that mission. Others simply avoid the topic of money altogether out of a fear or timidity with the topic in general. The reality is that "most churched people appreciate biblical teaching about their personal spiritual responsibilities—even those related to giving."[9]

Many individuals, who may not fall comfortably in one of the categories mentioned above, may still give to the organization if asked. Some individuals may be loosely connected to an organization, but still respond to a well-crafted passionate appeal or case statement. Others may be fully aware of the stellar reputation of the organization and give to it based upon that reputation if asked. Many organizations that include a self-addressed envelope in all of their communications receive "surprise donations" from individuals on a regular basis.

Even individuals who fall into one of the categories mentioned above must still be asked to contribute. Organizations cannot forget to "make the ask." If the leader of the organization is uncomfortable doing so, others should take on this task of inviting people to give. Many organizations have not because they ask not. It is entirely appropriate for an organization to demonstrate to its constituents detailed ways of how they can support the organization's mission.

Patterns of Giving

Even though there are many motivations to give, donors often follow certain patterns as they increase their giving. The goal of an organization should be to increase the level of involvement from each potential donor. If your organization does not currently have an annual appeal letter, I would suggest this as a place to start. The appeal letter should be given to a wide audience, detailing the most significant overall impacts of your mission every year. This type of appeal will obviously attract giving from your insiders, but will also set the stage for more dramatic appeals to other types of donors. Thus, you must track every response received. Sometimes, you will be able to discern who may be inclined to give to a particular cause from a note that they return or others may designate a response to a particular cause. As this happens, keep a list of people who may be "inclined" to give to a particular aspect of your mission and invite them to a dinner or reception to learn more about this one aspect. At the dinner, invite those impacted by your mission to tell their stories and encourage these people to "make the ask" so that others just like them may reap similar benefits.

Anyone who responds with a sizable check from your annual appeal should be thanked in person for his or her donation. Chances are that this person would like to make a more sizable "investment" or is looking for a way to express his or her gratitude stemming from an "indebtedness" to your organization. During the personal visit, take time to discover this person's particular interests. This may take more than one visit, as the potential donor takes time to get to know your organization better and as you take time to better understand this individual's desires and interests. Is this person inclined to give to a particular cause? Is the person interested in becoming an insider? What might the individual be likely to invest in?

Track all annual appeal responses and donations, looking for patterns or changes in giving. Someone who chooses not to give during a particular year is probably sending a message of dissatisfaction. Try to find out his or her story. There is always a story to be told, but sometimes it is a reluctant story.

Anyone who increases his or her donation is also sending a message and likewise has a story to tell. Ideally, the organization should keep a file on each potential donor, tracking patterns of giving, interests, and involvements with the organization. Different software packages are available to help track information about large sets of donors. Some are designed for particular types of organizations such as congregations or service organizations. Individual organizations that belong to a larger federation may have access to a larger national software program. Even for the small organization, a simple filing system or spreadsheet program will produce better results than no tracking at all. The only thing more important than remembering to ask someone to give is to remember to say "thank you" when he or she does.

Capacity and Balance

Most organizations require money. Leaders bring in money either from the products that they sell, the services that they provide, or the value that they instill in their members. As with other components of this model, there is a hierarchy to money. In businesses, people normally begin by purchasing one product, build a loyalty with that product, expand to other products, and eventually recruit other purchasers. With nonprofits, members normally begin by giving to a special request, expanding their giving into the annual fund or mission budget, contributing to a capital campaign, and finally bequesting a portion of their estates to the organization. Leaders in any organization must learn to cultivate such purchases or contributions.

Agile organizations also learn to balance the raising of money with the raising of goodwill. Organizations that "squeeze" out money from their customers or constituents can often improve their short-term outlook, but they destroy their long-term capacity. Even though organizations must never forget to "make the ask," the ask must be made with appropriate timing, care, and interest in the donor. The best fundraising stems from an initial friendship or relationship developed with the donor. Fundraising must be balanced with good public relations, integrity, and trust. Asked which side to tip the scale on this one, most leaders would probably tip on the money side. I always tip the scale toward goodwill. The balance that must be achieved in capacity building is the balance of raising dollars and raising goodwill.

CAPACITY POSTTEST

Please take a moment to revise your ranking of the following groups of givers to your organization in terms of how well your organization is doing connecting with each type of giver. Refine your rankings based upon your learnings and reflections. Remember that the categories are not meant to be mutually exclusive, meaning that some givers may fall into more than one category. Please rank the categories from 1 to 5, giving a "1" to the group that you are best connected with and a "5" to the group to which you are least connected.

_____ Insiders

_____ Inclined

_____ Investors

_____ Invited

_____ Indebted

CAPACITY DISCUSSION QUESTIONS

1. What are the allocations for which you must raise money in order to survive as an organization?
2. What are some items on your wish list?
3. How would the wish lists differ among your varying constituents?
4. Does your organization possess more of a scarcity mindset or an abundance mindset?
5. When was the last dramatic appeal made by your organization?
6. Which members of your organization are not afraid to ask people for money?
7. What fundraising strategies are you currently using?
8. How is your organization diversifying its appeals to your diversified constituency?
9. What patterns do your members follow as they increase giving to your organization?
10. What category would you add to the following list of types of donors: insiders, inclined, investors, indebted, and invited? Which group is the most difficult to appeal to in your organization?

MEASURING CAPACITY

For the following list of items, please indicate the extent to which you believe that your organization currently demonstrates these behaviors and activities according to the following schema. As you answer the questions, please draw upon your personal knowledge of your organization during the last six months. Please do not be afraid to use all parts of the spectrum in your responses. Total the responses for your "capacity" score.

5 = This is true of my organization almost all of the time
4 = This is true of my organization most of the time
3 = This is true of my organization about half the time
2 = This is seldom true of my organization
1 = I cannot recall a time when my organization did this

My organization...

_____ increases its budget every year.
_____ makes lots of friends.
_____ is good at fundraising.
_____ possesses a tremendous amount of goodwill in the community.
_____ seldom uses the word "scarcity" in regards to resources.
_____ would have many people reach out to help if it were in need.
_____ probably has many members who have named it as a benefactor in their wills.
_____ knows how to build good relationships with the community.
_____ never limits ideas because of funding.
_____ is liked in this community.

Total the scores for your capacity total _____.

Total the scores for 1, 3, 5, 7, and 9 _____. This represents your organization's ability to raise funds for its mission.

Total the scores for 2, 4, 6, 8, and 10 _____. This represents your organization's ability to raise goodwill.

8

Embracing Assets: *Allocations*

Capacity——Allocations
(strength)   (speed)

ALLOCATIONS PRETEST

No matter how well your organization has done with its fundraising, all future fundraising efforts will be directly influenced by how well you allocate the money that you have just raised. If donors suspect that the funds are not being handled properly, they will not give another dime. If they disagree with how the money is allocated, they will be more specific about the next dollar that they give. If they think that another organization is accomplishing your missional priorities with more impact or with more efficiency, they may give somewhere else. Fundraising is dependent upon how the income is distributed. In the pretest below, please rank the following aspects of allocation depending upon how well you believe that your organization is doing with each aspect. Please rank the categories from 1 to 4, giving a "1" to the aspect that you believe that your organization is handling the best and a "4" to the aspect that needs the most work in your organization.

_____ Integrity
_____ Involvement
_____ Information
_____ Influence

Allocations

One of my favorite stories related to allocating dollars stems from a local church that had raised money for eleven years just to replace the carpet throughout the building. They had actually completed several other emergency fundraising projects during those eleven years, but the carpet never rose to the same emergency status as the other projects. The carpet fund became a congregational icon. For eleven years, members pinched and saved in order to purchase the carpet. The trustees spent an additional year picking out the color. As a judicatory representative, I happened to be present on the day that the carpet was dedicated and was asked to give a prayer of dedication for the newly installed carpet. Indeed, there had been more planning put into the dedication service for the carpet installation than for most pastoral installations. Following the prayer, the chairperson of the trustees asked if he could make a special announcement regarding the carpet. I admit that I envisioned a long list of rules about preserving the carpet so that it might never have to be replaced again, or at least not within the lifetimes of any of the existing trustees. The chair arose to speak.

"It has taken us eleven years to raise funds for this carpet," he began. "And an additional year to ensure a proper color to coordinate with our other beautiful surroundings." There was a long pause. "Now," he continued, "Let's wear this carpet out to the glory of God!"

I was astounded. No long speech. No threats for anyone who dared spill something on the newly installed carpet. No warnings. No alarms. No alerts. No precautions. No blue ribbon rug commission and no clandestine floor covering watchdog unit. Just a simple encouragement to use the carpet that had been purchased with the giving of the members. This was a day that honored God.

This chapter is about allocating the money that an organization raises. Raising dollars and raising goodwill adds strength to the organization. Spending the money obviously adds speed to the organization as it is the allocations that drive the programs and the results. Your organization cannot hang onto its funds forever. The only reason that people give to an organization is to watch the organization spend the money that is given. In making allocations, however, the organization must be careful to balance short- and long-term expenditures.

Short- and Long-Term Allocations

Just as organizations need a short and long-term strategy for fundraising, they also need similar strategies for allocations. Most individuals set aside a portion of their paycheck to "run on" during the short term. Wise individuals also set aside some portion of their paycheck for longer-term needs or wants such as a maintenance fund, a vacation fund, or a Christmas fund. Many churchgoers operate on the 80–10–10 principle of saving ten percent of their income, giving ten percent of their income to their local church, and then operating on the other eighty percent. Whatever formula or plan is employed, both individuals and organizations need a short and long-term strategy. All organizations, profit and nonprofit alike, need to balance cash flow with long-term income producing assets.

Too often, organizations have nothing put away to help ensure their long-term viability. Others risk their very existence, over-protecting their long-term assets. Sometimes, organizations have unrestricted endowments that can be used for short-term needs, but they question whether or not to do so. If the monies given to such an endowment have been intended for the long-term health of the organization and traditionally only the interest has been used from such funds, then I suggest using those funds only under the following conditions: (1) If there is an opportunity to increase the long-term capacity of the organization through the strategic short-term use of those funds or (2) if the needs of the present generation are deemed to be greater than the needs of their grandchildren. Under the first condition, the withdrawal of funds should be made on a loaned basis with a repayment schedule included in the plan. Organizations need to balance short and long-term allocations. Both types, however, must also be allocated responsibly. It is to that end that we turn our attention next.

Responsible Allocations

People are watching how your organization spends its income. Making allocations appropriately greatly increases the likelihood of repeat donations. Making inappropriate allocations nearly guarantees that future fundraising efforts will fail. The four keys to making appropriate allocations are integrity, involvement, information, and influence.

Integrity

Those who make organizational decisions with respect to money play a fiduciary role. This means that they are responsible for making those decisions as if they were handling their own money. The integrity of the people in charge of the allocations has a direct relationship to giving. People will gauge the integrity of the organization by the integrity of its leaders. Everywhere we turn, people are pointing out poor financial practices that could lead to potential financial meltdowns.

In response to the Enron scandal, Congress passed a bill known as the Sarbanes Oxley legislation, which places increased accountability upon nonprofits and requires them to report income in a similar manner as for-profit companies. Your organization will want to make sure that it is in compliance with this act by consulting appropriate personnel such as an accounting firm or certified financial institution.

On a more practical note, I have listed below a checklist for you to review as a starting point to ensure that your organization is handling its money with integrity. This list of items is commonly called "internal controls." Internal controls, according to the National Center for Nonprofit boards, now called Boardsource, are policies, procedures, methods, and records designed by management to safeguard assets, generate reliable financial information, promote operational efficiency, and ensure adherence to policies. Here are some internal controls for you to review. How well does your organization fare on the list of practices below? I have included a blank line beside each item so you can check off the ones with which you are already in compliance.

_____ Establish written guidelines related to how you will handle the money for your organization.

_____ Always separate duties related to income and allocations. For instance, ask a financial secretary to oversee money that comes into the organization and a treasurer to oversee money that goes out of the organization. Staff or employees should not perform these duties.

_____ Always count money, such as income from church offerings or an event registration, immediately.

_____ Always have multiple people count the money. The people should also be unrelated to one another.

_____ Consider conducting background checks on the people who handle your money or ask them to be bonded. Some states may require this depending upon your organization.

_____ Deposit immediately. Never store money somewhere to be counted or deposited later.

_____ Always have an audit conducted of the accounting procedures. The type of audit should be commensurate with the size of the organization. Off-season audits can cost less. They are just as valid, but the timing of the findings may not fit as well into your overall financial planning strategy.

_____ Ask the board to adopt an annual budget detailing anticipated allocations. Set policies for how much deviation may be allowed from the budget prior to an additional vote of the board.

_____ Make a balance sheet and income statement available to the membership. A balance sheet can give a picture of your long-term assets. Income statements are a better indicator of cash flow.

_____ Always file tax reports on time. Remember that self-employed personnel must pay quarterly estimated income payments that include Social Security.

Involvement

While financial personnel carry a fiduciary responsibility for the organization, many organizations go beyond that and view their caretakers as stewards rather than merely overseers. The primary difference is derived from a level of involvement. Stewards are integrally involved with the organization so that they can make better financial decisions. They not only care for the money as if it were their own, they strive to care for the entire organization as if it were their own. The English word *steward* began to appear in manuscripts in the eleventh century. Early meanings of the word included, "an official who controls the domestic affairs of a household, supervising the service of his master's table, directing the domestics and regulating household expenditure; a major-domo."[1] The biblical roots of the word *oikonomos* are tied to our English word for economy. "Not only does this suggest that economics is a significant part of Christian stewardship; it means that what we call economics is more than the term regularly connotes in our vocabulary today!...stewardship has not only to do with money, budgeting, and finances, but with the whole ordering of our life, our corporate deployment of God's varied grace in the daily life of the world."[2]

Thus, those charged with oversight of finances are also by definition charged with oversight of the well-being of the organization. Just as it is impossible to separate finances from the rest of one's personal life, so it is with an organization. The more involved that the financial overseers become, the more sound financial decisions they will be able to make. One measure of involvement in the financial aspect of your organization is the extent to which those who handle your organization's finances see themselves as stewards of the well-being of your organization. The more the leaders perceive themselves to be stewards, the more they will act like stewards.

Stewards of an organization make their financial decisions in concordance with the values, mission, and vision of the organization. Those who make financial decisions must take time to equate themselves with the history, identity, hopes, and dreams of the organization in order to play their full stewardship role. "The church is a stewarding community... [T]heir whole life is to be an outpouring of God's varied grace."[3] In leading an organization, people practice stewardship in a variety of ways. Some things leaders steward by maintaining them in pristine condition, such as the buildings and grounds. Other items leaders steward by giving them away, such as the warmth and hospitality of the organization. Stewardship is always related to serving. "This process of emptying ourselves, thereby opening ourselves to a full recognition of God as Owner and Creator, is a significant part of the journey of the Christian Steward,"[4] Organizational leaders cannot simply take a few moments and read a balance sheet in order to be prepared to make financial decisions. They must take the time to understand the organization as an organism and nurture its health and growth. Agile organizations choose people who are involved in the life of the organization to handle their finances and they in turn seek to involve as many members as possible in the collection of the funds and the celebration of the results accomplished through those funds. Allocating money is an exciting time in the life of the organization to witness their funds at work.

Information

The sharing of financial information is a key piece in the allocation of an organization's resources. Occasionally, I encounter an organization in which a few key people have held the financial information for that organization for years, but they have been reticent to disclose it. Such a practice always leads to suspicion on the part of the members and constituents. Even though the people who control or account for the finances of an organization may exhibit the best intentions in their decision to limit access to the information, power within the organization becomes concentrated and centralized. When power is limited to a few, those giving up their power often feel a sense of forced compliance: "When we act to create compliance in others, we are choosing self-interest over service, no matter what words we use to describe our actions. Service-givers, who maintain dominance, aren't. Stewardship at the organizational level has to directly address the redistribution of power, and the redesign of fundamental management practices."[5] I believe that organizations should always err on the side of disclosure rather than discreteness in terms of their finances. Organizations in sound financial condition will be seen as good stewards. Those concerned that donors may not give because the organization "has too much in the bank" can always dream bigger dreams to match their financial condition.

On the other hand, organizations that are concerned about disclosing "too little in the bank" will be rewarded for presenting an honest picture. It is true that no one wants to give to a sinking ship, but donors can be influenced to give to a struggling organization with a hopeful and viable plan for the future. Organizations experiencing financial difficulty will benefit as well from the suggestions and ideas of their fellow stewards. Contributors who later discover that an organization is in worse shape financially than originally disclosed will feel duped by the leaders and will be much more tentative about future giving. It is not good to withhold information that constituents feel they have a right to know. "They must have something to hide," ponder potential donors, "otherwise the information would be in the public domain."

Influence

Donors want to know that their organization is making a difference in the world. Organizations with a strong mission will have a much easier time in encouraging people to hand over their hard-earned dollars to that mission. Lack of mission, on the other hand, leads to a lack of dollars. Clarity is the key in both the raising and allocating of dollars. This is true for all nonprofit organizations, but is especially true for local churches: "For a century and a half at least, stewardship and mission have been linked in the life of the church. The uncertainty about stewardship so widespread these days is really in large part an uncertainty about mission."[6]

Those responsible for the oversight of finances should demonstrate how the dollars given translate into mission. An organization that feeds the hungry should be aware of how many children can be fed with a one dollar donation. An organization that supplies beds for the homeless should be aware of how many comfortable nights' rest can be bought with a single donation. Schools and colleges should know how much is spent on each student. People want to influence the mission with their dollars. The closer that the connection between donations and mission can be made in the donor's mind, the more likelihood the donor will give in the future.

Sometimes, donors want to know who is involved in the actual distribution of the dollars as one gauge of knowing that their interest in allocation matches the allocations of the organization. This is often an interest within ethnic organizations. Givers want to know that their interests are represented. One way of doing this is to ensure that the same ethnic balance is achieved among those distributing the dollars as in those giving the dollars: "The amount of giving to the black church is a sign of trust in an institution that historically has been controlled by African Americans. I cannot emphasize enough the importance of control to black donors; the question of which entity controls the allocation of charitable dollars is a central one."[7]

Allocations with Movements and Institutions

All institutions must guard against overemphasizing the maintenance of the institution over the mission of the institution. In a recent study from the *Pulpit and Pew Project*, "Keeping the doors open" was the number one concern in congregations of less than one hundred active members.[8] While those who practice stewardship for an organization as its board of trustees or its board of directors must be concerned about maintaining a structure to carry out the mission, sometimes those leaders are tempted to confuse the maintenance of their own roles with the maintenance of the institution. At this point, it is helpful to clarify that while the stewardship of an organization is a critical role, ultimately those individuals do not own the organization itself.

Stewards of movements envision a future of the organization that extends beyond their leadership, and envision new leaders who can advance the organization beyond their own limitations in the future. Leaders tread into dangerous waters when they begin to believe that no one else can lead the organization quite like them. When that happens, it is impossible to make wise decisions about the efficiency or even downsizing of the infrastructure of the organization, even when that may be called for by other factors under consideration. The breadth and depth of an organization should expand and contract with the development of its programs. Sometimes an organization must embrace the developing stage while at other times it must activate the delivery stage in order to meet the demands of its constituents.

Stewards must always guard against serving their own interests: "The steward exists not only to serve his or her master, but in doing so to serve as well those whose interests the master has at heart. When stewards begin to allow their own ambition or desire to dictate what should be done, they at once disqualify themselves."[9] Servants and stewards of God's mission must serve God's people. Stewards of movements rather than institutions are willing to transform all of the organization's assets into new forms and structures in order to advance a more important mission in the future. Even if it means selling land, unrestricting funds, redirecting assets, or abandoning programming to embrace new possibilities, stewards of movements are willing to do whatever is required to keep the movement going. Sometimes speeding up the movement means casting off items from the hot air balloon so that it can rise higher and further than ever before. Stewards of movements are just as concerned about the future of the organization as they are about its present-day activities.

Allocations in Unexpected Times

One of the best ways to discover what a person is truly like is to observe the person under a great amount of stress. Stories often circulate of how professional interviewers have fictitiously told the interviewee that he or she had arrived on the wrong date for the interview just to observe the response. Others interviewers have given a sample project to potential employees to see how they respond to "on the spot" project development. Interview questions that deal with hypothetical situations are also becoming increasingly popular with search committees. Just as we can discern a great deal from observing an *individual* under pressure, so can we detect the priorities of an *organization* by examining how it responds under pressure.

Unexpected Income

Remember that organizations are also organisms. They have all of the dynamics of an individual. Thus, one of the best ways to unearth more about an organization is to observe what it does with either unexpected income or unexpected debt. This is also a great question to ask of your leaders and members. Hypothetically, what would your organization do with $50,000 of unexpected income? Take a moment now to jot down your answer below:

A group of seventy-five congregations gave the answers listed below. The answers are given in descending order of popularity.[10] How does your answer compare with the list below?

- Place the funds in an endowment.
- Apply the funds to a special local program.
- Use the funds to reduce a debt.

- Purchase some special equipment.
- Use the funds for a special maintenance project.
- Invest the money in a church account, but give away the interest every year.
- Give the entire amount to a worthy cause.
- Use the money for current expenses.

Unexpected Debt

Now, ponder what your organization would cut if you incurred an unexpected debt. Suppose your building sustained wind damage that was not completely covered by insurance and you had recently exhausted your reserves. Which program, person, or project would you let go? Once again, take a moment to jot down your own answer prior to reading the responses below. The responses again come from Loyde Hartley, given in descending order.[11] Again, how do your answers compare to Hartley's list?

- Support for projects outside of the congregation.
- Funds sent to the denomination.
- Maintenance of buildings.
- Educational programming.
- Staff salaries other than the pastor.
- Debt-reduction payments.
- Pastoral salary.

Allocations and Balance

As leaders leverage assets that have been acquired in the organization, they must balance expenditures and investments. *Expenditures* consist of those items that are necessary to maintain the organization. *Investments* consist of those items that potentially will yield further assets in the future. Thriving businesses achieve a balance between production costs and research and development. Thriving nonprofits achieve a balance between maintaining their services and investing in training their personnel. This will potentially lead to increased cooperation or added services. Certainly the endowments of an organization must be viewed primarily from the investment rather than the expenditures side. Both yield different forms of leveraging.

Agile organizations balance their tangible assets with their intangible assets as they learn to balance fundraising with goodwill (from the capacity chapter). Paying attention to the tangibles of the organization, such as money and expenses, is an example of a coincident pattern in the organization. In order to be maintained, the tangibles must be cared for, checked on, and nurtured. Giving attention to the intangibles, such as goodwill and investments, is an example of a temporal pattern. Enhancing goodwill and seeking a quality return on investments is something that demands a constant looking ahead to discover what needs might be attended to by the organization's members and personnel. If this tension between tangibles and intangibles is not balanced within the organization, it could lead to its demise. Although the pathways to destruction vary, an organization can do itself in by overemphasizing money over goodwill or expenses over investments. Likewise, it can meet its demise by emphasizing goodwill over money and investments over expenditures. Either will yield an obsolete organization. Organizations that expend all of their money in current programming will one day find themselves outdated, being out of touch with the next demand that has surfaced. On the other hand, organizations that spend too much time developing programs will find that the perfect program that they have developed is of interest only to a generation that lived ten or fifteen years ago. Agile organizations find a way to balance tangibles and intangibles.

ALLOCATIONS POSTTEST

Please take a moment to revise your ranking of the following aspects of allocations depending upon how well you believe that your organization is doing with each aspect. Please rank the categories from 1 to 4, giving a "1" to the aspect that you believe that your organization is handling the best and a "4" to the aspect that needs the most work in your organization. Refine your original list as needed based upon your learnings and reflections from this chapter.

_____ Integrity
_____ Involvement
_____ Information
_____ Influence

ALLOCATIONS DISCUSSION QUESTIONS

1. How do the members of your organization treat tangible assets such as carpet and refrigerators? Are they happy to wear them out or do they restrict their use?
2. Does your organization have more short-term or long-term funds? How does this influence decision-making?
3. What recent financial disasters can you recall from recent news stories?
4. Has your organization put into place sufficient internal controls to avoid a financial disaster of your own?
5. Who is more involved in your organization, those who give the money or those who spend it?
6. What pieces of financial information are you curious about in your organization? How could you discover those answers?
7. Who are the stewards of your organization?
8. What would your organization do with unexpected income?
9. What would your organization curtail if required to do so by lack of income?
10. How well are you balancing expenditures and investments?

MEASURING ALLOCATIONS

For the following list of items, please indicate the extent to which you believe that your organization currently demonstrates these behaviors and activities according to the following schema. As you answer the questions, please draw upon your personal knowledge of your organization during the last six months. Please do not be afraid to use all parts of the spectrum in your responses. Total the responses for your "allocations" score.

5 = This is true of my organization almost all of the time
4 = This is true of my organization most of the time
3 = This is true of my organization about half the time
2 = This is seldom true of my organization
1 = I cannot recall a time when my organization did this

My organization...

_____ handles its expenditures and income separately.
_____ is not afraid to put its resources to good use.
_____ always receives a clean audit.
_____ uses its resources in ways that build more resources.
_____ has many donors who trust it to make good financial decisions.
_____ makes good investments.
_____ never spends money inappropriately.
_____ is not afraid to take risks with its assets.
_____ has a fair budgeting process.
_____ tries to discover new uses for its existing assets.

Total the scores for your allocations total _____.

Total the scores for 1, 3, 5, 7, and 9 _____. This represents your organization's ability to make good expenditures.

Total the scores for 2, 4, 6, 8, and 10 _____. This represents your organization's ability to invest in its own future.

9

Embracing Change: *Passion*

Passion——Maturity
(strength)   (speed)

Everywhere we turn, we encounter forces encouraging us to change. Magazine articles challenge our organizations to add new programs. Global warming issues challenge us to understand our ecology. Competitors remind us to update our technology. Plus, we have our own dreams and goals for the future. In the spaces below, take some time to list the changes that your organization is currently being challenged to consider.

Now, take a look at items that you have listed. Place the letter "S" beside any item that you believe is "still" influencing your organization and the letter "A" beside items that you believe are "already" beginning to influence your organization toward change.

Some items may contain neither marking. What percentage of S's and A's did you mark?

_____ Still   _____Already

Change

Your organization will have little strength for change until it discovers its passion for change. While serving as a youth minister several years ago, sometimes a parent would visit my office asking that I "do something" about their child's behavior. After several unsuccessful and naïve attempts to encourage unwanted change in someone else's life, I came to the conclusion that no one can force anyone else to change. This includes parents, counselors, teachers, mentors, parole officers, wardens, and it even includes leaders of organizations. Leaders cannot force an organization to change unless the organization itself has a passion to do so. Understanding that passion adds an amazing degree of strength to the organization, revolutionizing the change process altogether. Once understood, the change process shifts from one of motivating others toward harnessing the power and the drive to change.

This chapter addresses all types of change, including the most difficult, a wholesale change of either the identity or vision of the organization. Whatever the intended change, passion is the key to making it a reality. Certainly leaders can implement an occasional new program or rally their staff to adopt a new policy without discovering the passion of the organization. But, even those changes will be implemented more smoothly if the leaders can tap into fervor for the fine-tuning. Even goal substitution, when autocratic or charismatic leaders replace the existing priorities of an organization with new ones, will benefit from galvanizing enthusiasm for the new direction. An organization will not convert unless it has a passion to do so.

With that in mind, we now begin to explore the various sources or drivers of potential change in organizations. The drivers come from three primary directions: namely, the contour of the environment, the competition of the market, and the collisions of existing personnel. It is important to identify the sources of change for several reasons, but the obvious is perhaps the most important: "Identifying the source of the pressure to make the change helps you answer the question in almost every employee's mind: Why are we making this change anyway?"[1] Until the passion is identified, there will be no answer to the *why* question, and answering that question is critical to implementing change.

Changes Driven by Environmental Contour

Agile organizations stay abreast of local and global trends that could potentially impact those organizations. Their leaders track newspaper articles, read editorials, join the chamber of commerce, participate in on-line chats, read literature outside of their trade field, and regularly engage in discussions about the global milieu. Agile organizations are permeable. Information flows both in and out of the organization to other organizations and other cultures. Organizations that ignore the outside world will find themselves living alone someday. The world is changing too fast for organizations or even departments within an organization to act independently of others. Organizations intent on canvassing the contour have a team of people focused outside the organization. Tracking the environment is not an extra or a bonus. It is an essential part of survival and growth for every organization in today's chaotic world.

There are even trends in tracking trends. Some trend watchers suggest that, increasingly, number crunchers and trends watchers will replace intuition among organizational leaders. Ian Ayres, one of those trend watchers, has identified a trend that may affect organizations for years to come: "the replacement of expertise and intuition by objective, data-based decision making, made possible by a virtually inexhaustible supply of inexpensive information. Those who control and manipulate this data will be the masters of the new economic universe."[2] Ayres demonstrates how his theory is already beginning to change our world:

> Amazon's® computers know what we'll like even before we figure it out for ourselves... Netflix® customers like the movies the service recommends better than the ones they choose on their own... Auto dealers use the same kinds of data to calculate to a fine point just how far they can push their customers on price and loan rates. When airlines cancel a flight, they use an algorithm to predict which customers are most vulnerable to being lured away by a competitor and give them, not the airline's own best customers, priority in rebooking.[3]

This information suggests that, in addition to reading newspapers and trade magazines, you might want to network with others who are doing so or join an organization of futurists who study horizons for a living in order to tap trend experts.

Obviously, it is impossible to scan every available trend that might affect your organization, but doing something is preferable to doing nothing. As you begin to look for trends, you will be amazed at how quickly patterns develop. Your interests will also quickly gravitate toward those arenas that effect your organization. Some places are more prone to patterns than others. For instance, external factors that almost always drive organizational change include trends in capital, currency fluctuations, business cycles, interest rates, political landscapes, changes in labor supply and demand, intellectual property laws, tariffs, affirmative action, NAFTA, the Americans with Disabilities Act, and industry regulation/deregulation.[4] Additionally, I discuss below some broader trends that may affect your organization in the future, or at least present opportunities for it. In addition to the more detailed aspects of environmental change, such as interest rates and hog futures, often broad landscape changes can affect organizational change. Below are some current trends at work in the environmental contour.

Demographics

While Japan and much of Western Europe are declining in population, every U.S. census taken since 1790 has shown a population increase. It took the United States 139 years to get to 100 million people, 52 years to add the next million, and just 39 years after that to add the last 100 million.[5] Not all sections of the United States, however, are experiencing the same rate of growth, and a few areas are not growing at all. The last several decades have given rise to a great shift in populated areas. As a result, the scale has been tipped; now more than one-half of the U.S. population lives in the South and the West. The five fastest growing states, percentage-wise, from 1990 to 2000 were Nevada (66 percent), Arizona (44 percent), Colorado (31 percent), Utah (30 percent), and Idaho (29 percent). One of the more intriguing shifts relates to the impact of water on land holdings. The Pareto principle now applies to land and water: more than one half of the population lives on the 20 percent of land that is within fifty miles of the major bodies of water adjacent to the U.S., namely the Atlantic, Pacific, Gulf, and Great Lakes.

In terms of age, the U.S. has been working on an hourglass figure. In 1990 the U.S. median age was 22.9 and today it is 36.5 and rising.[6] But, this is a misleading statistic because fewer and fewer people fall into what we call middle age. Baby Boomers are turning 60 and their children are only in their thirties or younger, as many Baby Boomers waited longer to have their first child. This has resulted in a gap of middle-aged and working class people. In 1960, one half of the U.S. households had children in them and today only a third of them do.

For the next several years, the largest group by far will be the retired. One-half of the people who have ever lived past the age of 65 are still breathing today. Some readers are obviously more grateful for this statistic than others. By 2030, 20 percent of Americans will probably be over the age of 65. Today, there are about 50,000 centenarians. By 2050 turning "100" will become even more common, as those who do will have more than one million friends who can claim the same milestone. In a few years, the retiree population will be growing faster than the population in any state in the United States.

We have all heard about the potential effects of the hourglass on Social Security, healthcare, prescription drugs, etc. What impact will it have on your organization? The aging population brings with it challenges as well as opportunities. Many new retirees are looking for a significant volunteer experience. They do not want to stuff envelopes or fold newsletters. They crave real job descriptions that come with an opportunity to make a real difference in the community. One of the myths about age is that only young people join causes. Young people and newly retired are equally strong sources of recruitment. In terms of years to give, a teenager is only so for seven years, and will likely shift interests in his or her twenties. Someone who turns sixty-five can anticipate continuing to live nearly three times as long as that. In terms of congregations, research shows that individuals join congregations in similar percentages at every stage of life. Congregations who offer growth opportunities for every stage of life rather than targeting a narrow age cohort are usually pleased with the results.

Age is not the only variable in which a shift has been occurring within the U.S. population. Ethnicity is another place that has witnessed dramatic shifts. Today, ten states no longer have a white majority. By 2016, minorities will comprise one third of the U.S. population. The foreign-born population has increased in every single state since 1990, and more than doubled in all but seventeen states. The last five years alone have seen a 16 percent increase in the number of immigrants living in the U.S.[7] While many congregations, service organizations, and other institutions lament over a decline in membership, the best predictor of church membership is the birthrate of whites in the U.S. from 1950 to the present day. I suspect that this correlation may be true of other types of organizations. Mainline congregations grew by appealing to the immigrant populations of the twentieth century. There was absolutely no reason why U.S. congregations should have declined, if they had continued to reach out to immigrant populations. But today, attitudes have shifted. Only 49 percent of people in the U.S. feel that immigrants have a positive effect on the country (compared to 77 percent among Canadians). Certainly, immigration is a topic that has captured media attention. How well has your local church, school, or service organization helped your members or students to understand the various issues involved? How have you responded to the needs of your most recent new neighbors?

Technology

How well is your organization using technology? Even if you have not done very well on this front, evidence suggests that the best opportunities in this arena are yet to come. From a global perspective, only about 15 percent of the world's population is connected to the Internet, but this figure could rise to 50 percent over the next fifteen years. Running technology also requires energy. The demand for energy could also increase by 50 percent over the same period. The use of technology will increasingly mean that the older will learn from the younger. How often do you provide opportunities for that to take place in your organization? The half-life of knowledge is only about five years, so if the opportunities are not there, it means that the organization is not only growing distant from its employees, but from its environment as well.

Does technology have any limits? We only have to ask ourselves if we envisioned computers in cars, toasters, microwaves, watches, eyeglasses, hearts, and keychains to answer that question. Where will the latest technology take us into the future? How about into two places at one time? Cloning is flying under the radar, with the exception of those directly involved in stem cell research, as well as methods that use a person's own DNA to manufacture new organs.

Debt

Do you know the last year that Americans made more money than they spent? It was 1933. Does that year ring any bells? In 2005, Americans in the U.S. spent forty-one billion dollars more than they made. One of the major contributors to expanding debt is that people launch their careers with more of it. Student loans have increased by 27 percent since 1998 and today's average student graduates with $17,000 in loans. And now the housing bubble has burst. Once housing prices turn downward it is difficult to turn around. The average home price in Japan has dropped every year since it began its downward trend fourteen years ago.

As I said earlier, there are even trends among those who identify trends. One of those discoveries comes from the theory of emergence. It is an idea that suggests that trends may be much less orchestrated than we think, and thus much less controllable. In his book *Emergence*, Stephen Johnson shows how broad historical patterns have a way of repeating themselves. He demonstrates how cities were formed with amazing similarity with no global communication: "There are patterns of human movement and decision-making that have been etched into the texture of city blocks, patterns that are then fed back to the residents themselves, altering their subsequent decisions... You don't need regulations and city planners deliberately creating these structures. All you need are thousands of individuals and a few simple rules of interaction."[8] Similar emergent patterns are described among ants that have no queen ant or form of central communication, among our human immune systems, the stock market, and in our World Wide Web. Emergence theory suggests that some environmental changes may be too large to control, where the only choice is whether to get on board, or buy the burial plot for our outmoded organization, another reason to stay abreast of the contour.

In addition to tracking trends that may potentially affect all organizations, another reason for studying the environmental contour is to discover opportunities unique to the organization's needs and assets. Organizations that limit their study of the outside world to the study of similar organizations never capitalize on trends that only they might embrace because of their unique position. For instance, during the 1950s nearly every church in America added an educational wing for the promotion of Sunday school classes. Now, many of those wings stand empty because the patterns of small groups have shifted. Many would love to have some of that space for parking as the trend of mobility increased. Imagine if a few of those churches had rented space or partnered with others to create common educational offerings rather than constructing buildings on space they could not afford. The ones who did so might have been well on their way to embracing the next trend that came along, that of networking with others both on-line and face to face. They would have still responded to the trend of increasing their educational offerings, but in a way that suited them. If you think such insight is impossible to foresee, consider the actions of a farmer friend of mine who stored the grain that the government paid him to store in a newly built warehouse that he built rather than grain elevators. When the government contracts dried up, he sold the warehouse for a profit as well. There is no substitute for studying the contour and contemplating how the patterns that you see might affect the mission that you embrace. It is also wise, however, to take a look at what organizations similar to yours are doing. We turn our attention toward the competition.

Changes Driven by Competition

What is your neighbor organization up to these days? Knowing may mean the difference between your organization *thriving* or *surviving*. Organizations can benefit greatly from studying their potential competition or by studying similar organizations whose results they desire to have as well. The more an organization studies its competition, the more options it will have. This is because no change occurs in isolation. Changes are complementary. Make a change in one area, such as adding a new employee or changing the incentive system, and it will affect other parts of the organization. Making a major change in one arena can even compensate for the lack of change in another. The irony of change is that the more changes that become available to an organization, the fewer alterations it will have to endure because it can zero in on those with the most leverage.

Agile organizations select key changes to embrace; they don't just change for the sake of change. We have all met leaders who tend to adopt every new idea that comes along. The current organizational redeemer for their organizations is always the most recent idea to appear in *Fortune, Fast Company,* or *Wired,* or the latest idea to surface from a recently attended conference. Think for a moment about these kind of people who you have met. Do they lead agile organizations? Chances are they lead chaotic organizations, but, while chaos is sometimes necessary, it does not automatically translate into agility without a plan. An organization should study what similar organizations are up to, but it need not embrace every new opportunity that comes along. Doing so will lessen trust from constituents. Both those within and outside the organization will have trouble buying into the latest idea if the previous one was not implemented successfully. A brand new leader has "chips to expend" because no new idea has yet failed. But, the first time that one does, the leader must choose carefully and complete the implementation of the next theory, not just consume people's time exploring the notion of it.

One of the ways to have more options at your disposal is to involve as many people as possible in studying similar organizations. If a single person is designated to "build strategic relationships" or "network" the organization with others, the options for change will be limited to the mind of that single individual. What if the person misses a major opportunity? On the other hand, if everyone in the organization has one eye toward the environment, seeking positive opportunities for change (in addition to keeping an eye on their tasks at hand), then the organization will have multiple opportunities from which to choose. Agile organizations often delegate certain types of similar organizations for the staff to study. Organizations aware of only one new idea will have only one option. Organizations aware of the plethora of opportunities can choose to embrace the changes that best suit them.

Below, I list a few trends that are taking place in organizations that may be similar to yours. I encourage you to visit other churches, schools, service organizations, etc., in order to discover the best practices of others in your field. Take advantage of such opportunities while on vacation, traveling for the organization, or even on-line through virtual tours. Have fun discovering what your neighbor may be up to. One of the myths of studying similar organizations is that they may be reluctant to share "trade secrets." Certainly this would be true in some organizations, such as those who chase patents and develop technology. But, among most nonprofits, I have found a willingness to share best practices with others. Most are honored to be asked to share a principle or strategy that has worked for them.

The Workplace

Creativity, compassion, and cultural creation are a few aspects that increasingly define jobs in the workplace. Scott Adams (creator of *Dilbert*) says, "The only people who will have jobs in the U.S. are people with creative jobs, or something that has to do with communications and sales, and more people are going to work at home,"[9] People are searching for meaningful work, often characterized by variety. Excellence no longer has the sole toehold on satisfaction. People also want their work to be ethical and even altruistic. They want to make a difference. Certainly congregations and many other nonprofits have an opportunity to model what it means to be a part of a meaningful organization and many are doing so. Jack Carroll reports, "Shaping Congregational Culture is increasingly seen as a task of the pastor. A pastor helps to 'produce' or at least decisively shape a congregation's culture."[10]

Creativity and compassion, however, must also be balanced with practicality. Another new aspect of workplace culture is the linkage of new ideas with marketing. From the genesis of an idea, many businesses consider how to gain ownership of the idea or how to advertise it to their constituents and customers. Tim Brown, CEO of Ideo, comments, "In the future, designers are going to have to be much more sophisticated when they're conceiving new ideas and think about how they're going to speak to the market and how their ideas are going to contribute to marketing rather than just sending it down the line."[11] For nonprofits, this translates into, "For an idea to have merit is must be feasible and be easy to implement in addition to being worthy."

Transparency

The demand for stronger financial internal controls has also led to a demand for increased transparency in organizations. John Mackey, CEO, Whole Foods Market, Austin, Texas, writes, "You are going to have to assume that everything is an open book. When there are fewer secrets, there will be more motivation to do the right thing. I think this is part of a larger trend, toward business having a greater responsibility than just maximizing profits. People want businesses to be good citizens, but not all are getting it."[12]

Transparency is not just demanded from businesses, it is becoming a part of the society in general. Private conversations are wiretapped with no warrant to do so, photos are taken of your walk in the park, and DNA is documented for future years. We are becoming increasingly accustomed to sharing more and more personal information.

Choice, Expansion, and Demand for Quality

We all have experienced the penchant for choice in today's world. Crayons have expanded from eight to sixty-four colors. A good ice cream store must have *at least* thirty-one flavors. While eating at a restaurant the other day, I embarrassed my family once again by pointing out to the server that the 84 combinations that they claimed were possible to make from their appetizer, main course, and dessert options were actually 218. Choice sometimes increases by the minute.

People want choices and, ideally, they would like to be able to find all of those choices under one roof. The demand for bigger and better is all around us. With its rapid expansion through the last several decades, Wal-Mart® now employs as many people as our public K-12 schools. While we have always had megachurches, there has been a dramatic rise in them ever since efficiency and quality became a standard concern in corporations. Churches that strive to provide all things to all people must have the means, and megachurches certainly have more means than others, thus the reason for their rapid growth. Others are simply going to have to provide some of the things to some of the people with more care and greater focus. While the average congregation contains about one hundred active members, 50 percent of the people who worship on any given Sunday are in congregations of four hundred members and above. To put it another way, if both of the neighbors on either side of you go to church, one of them will be in a church of at least four hundred worshipers. Cross-congregational conversations about the quality of worship and expectations of programming will probably only serve to increase this trend.

With the rise of bigger and better has come increased pressure upon CEOs to produce it. Even though the average Fortune 500 Company spends two million dollars on a CEO search, 50 percent of them are gone in the first eighteen months. Many CEOs and other organizational leaders bemoan unrealistic expectations. Unless clarified, expectations can present an unrealistic scenario for leaders. It is impossible to meet all of the demands expressed by the members of many organizations. All organizations need to be aware of the trend toward bigger and better, but not all organizations can go there. Most simply need to clarify their niche, their mission, their vision, and their expectations rather than aiming at degrees of expansion beyond the realm of the feasible.

Challenging Tradition

Traditions are not what they used to be. When the current generation receives the answer of, "Because we have always done it that way," to their question of, "Why do we do it this way?" the answer does not suffice. If traditions remain important, it is because we choose them all over again. Jack Carroll writes, "Posttraditional society does not mean the end of tradition. It means instead a world in which traditions can be claimed, rejected, reinterpreted, or even invented, but not simply taken for granted and uncritically followed." Authority is not "out there" in the tradition, but "in here" in our experience as disembedded, mobile selves who must therefore become authors of our own identities.

How have some of the workplace and organizational changes listed above affected your church, school, or service organization? How have you responded to the demand for choice? Have you experienced a push toward the bigger and better? Have you seen a decrease in traditions? How have you responded to these shifts? Before you linger too long on this particular issue, there is one more source of change yet to consider. The first two sources originate outside of the organization. The third source originates from within.

Changes Driven by Collisions

People within an organization often quarrel over who has the real power to lead, who should be making decisions over what, how to best serve the needs of the constituents, whom to call or hire, and whether or not to upgrade equipment and data systems such as communication and information systems. Collisions occur when members disagree about practices, priorities, and public statements. They are common in most organizations. These collisions can provide insight into the passion for change present in an organization. Opportunistic collisions can occur over organizational identity, values, ethics, preferences, and organizational positions. Agile organizations view conflict as yet one more opportunity to change for the better.

When internal collisions occur, the organization has three primary options. The leaders can let the majority rule. They can favor the side most aligned with their current organizational culture. Or they can seek to transform the organization into one that can handle the seemingly opposing viewpoints. For now, I simply want to explain how to identify collisions that may serve as sources of organizational passion.

Sources of Collision That May Lead to a Passion to Change

Collisions slow an organization down. Organizations hit the pause button in order to assess a conflict. While dealing with a conflict, the organization expends opportunities. But, once the issues related to the conflict have been identified, the organization has an unique opportunity that extends well beyond hitting the play button and returning to normal functioning. Sometimes, one or more of the parties involved in the conflict bring to the surface a change that the entire organization should address. Issues of disagreement often speak to values, perspectives, and ideology, all of which can become rich fodder for organizational change. Certainly, some personnel collisions are nothing more than personality conflicts, but other types of collisions among members signal an opportunity for the organization to go in a new direction. Typically, there are three places to look for such changes: namely, collisions over leadership, values, and technology.

Members disagree over leadership in a variety of ways. They may disagree over who should be leading the organization. They may disagree over the priorities set by the leaders. They may disagree with the strategies adopted by the leaders. Regardless of the type of disagreement, disputes over leadership often signal an opportunity for organizational growth. Strong leaders do not shun or stifle those who disagree with them. They seek to understand the reasons behind the disagreement and leverage the passion within it. Leaders of agile organizations consistently search for new perspectives.

When pastoring a church several years ago, I had been extremely cautious in suggesting any radical changes; even ones that I felt might greatly benefit the church. I had been especially cautious among the older members of the congregation. One day one of these members came to me and said, "Where are all of those ideas that people said that you had? We are ready for them." When I explained my cautiousness, the member countered and called my bluff, suggesting that we conduct a survey to try to uncover some of the attitudes toward change in the congregation. The member was right. There was actually a greater desire for change among the longer tenured members of the congregation than among the newer members. There was a passion for newness that I had been blind to because of my thoughts of cautiousness.

Collisions over customer or constituent values may also signal a rising passion for organizational change. Some staff may want to pay more attention to what the customers (or those being served by the organization) want, while others may believe that their track record proves that they are in touch with the customers. Some may resist customer information because they fear being asked to develop new skills or adopt new practices. Typically, disputes over customer needs indicate an opportunity for organizational change. Good news. This type of collision is among the easiest to resolve. The way to resolve this one is to ask the customers what they want.

A third source of opportunistic collision relates to changes in technology. When someone within the organization is either pushing for newer technology or resisting the opportunity to learn about technology, this usually signals an opportunity for change throughout the organization. Technology can be a frightening phenomenon, but is always a necessary one. Embracing or shunning technology often separates today's organizations. Agile organizations do not go out and buy the latest gadget because it is new, but they do track new products and resources that can enhance their mission and vision.

In addition to identifying some potential sources of organizational passion within the content of the collisions, I also want to highlight a few trends that are occurring among the nature of the collisions themselves. Recently, internal collisions have become more violent, more specific to particular individuals, and are occurring among newer rather than older members of an organization.

Violence in Organizations

One of the trends in organizational culture is that collisions are becoming increasingly violent. Chances are that you know someone personally who has been trained in mediation. Chances are that such a mediator can cite several examples of individuals threatening one another in an escalated dispute. It may get worse before it gets better according to a trend spotter at Bendixen & Associates. In December of 2006, the firm conducted a survey of 600 people from the ages of 16–22 inquiring about their career plans: "Almost 70 percent said they'd be working in a specific career, 12 percent said they'd be in a university, and an additional 1 percent said the military. And, like a bolt from the blue, a significant number [of those planning to go into the military] volunteered that they'd most likely be military snipers! For every respondent who says something spontaneously, several more are thinking it."[13] The researcher made the metaphorical leap that you are probably making as well. "It's also a symbol of the way people like to operate in this country. Politicians face 'snipers' every day who are trying to find one out-of-place word to put on YouTube. In this country, stealth is in."[14] Internal revolutionaries are rising. In my work in organizational development, I have seen a dramatic change in the language used by conflicted parties, the practices they employ to make their points, and in the destruction they are willing to inflict upon the opposition.

Mavens and Ravens

Not all insiders carry equal weight when it comes to influencing organizational change. Nearly every organization contains members who spend much more time and energy relating to a broader set of individuals within the organization than anyone else. Over the years, I have observed that these individuals come in two forms: namely, mavens and ravens. The primary difference lies in the motivations of the two. Mavens are driven by an intense desire to help others. Ravens are driven by an intense desire to satisfy an internal need. Mavens have a need to share information; ravens have a need to consume it. Mavens typically mean well, ravens don't always.

Malcolm Gladwell reintroduced the term "maven" into the mainstream in *The Tipping Point*. He identified mavens as those who control knowledge by accumulating it. For Gladwell, the key to mavens is that they want to help for no other reason than because they like to help.[15] They have no hidden agenda. They do not impose their own dreams on others. They have an innate desire to help others achieve their own desires. Thus, they contain the key ingredient to friendship: trust. Because mavens are so trusted in organizations, they can have a huge influence on the changes that organizations embrace. An agile organization knows where the mavens are within it.

Given their sphere of influence, mavens can wield a great deal of influence in an organization. The good news is that they are typically motivated by positive values. The bad news is that there is another type of individual in organizations who seeks to gather lots of information. However, he or she is typically motivated by either an entrepreneurial attitude or revenge, not altruism. I call these individuals "ravens." Some ravens are seeking to build their own kingdoms. Other ravens have been burned by the organization and want to see it fail by suggesting specific changes perceived to be impossible to embrace. Both mavens and ravens may call for the same type of change within an organization, but be motivated by different passions. More typically, several ravens will band together and seek change or even take over, often each with differing motivations camaflouged by a unifying demand. One way to spot a group of ravens is when you observe people having frequent conversations who previously had little to talk about. Responding to ravens and mavens involves the same technique espoused throughout this chapter: namely, seeking to discover the passion behind their suggestions and leveraging that passion toward positive change. Even if the specific change seems unrealistic, try to discover the passion that can be channeled into a more positive outcome.

Collisions Initiated by the Newest Members

Another type of collision may occur between someone new to the organization and one its pillars. People with a blank page or a fresh look often think very differently about the organization than someone steeped in its bylaws. Liz Nickles writes:

> There was the notion that you have to pay your dues, you have to be isolated in your corporate silo, and then—eventually—you'll get to join the club and actually get to do some interesting work for a change. It's incredible how that worked. And it's not happening any more. The curtain has been pulled back and people actually understand that there is some virtue to inexperience, and inexperienced people often do some amazing things.[16]

As organizations embrace more opportunities and experience more change, one of the trends is that newer members increasingly conflict with longer tenured members. Agile organizations find a way to listen to all of the sources of passion signaling potential change, even sources that may be brand new to the organization.

Passion within Movements and Institutions

Movements differ from institutions in many ways. With respect to change, movements differ from institutions by viewing change as commonplace. Institutions often create restructuring committees to deal with change. Movements are so accustomed to change that they have no need of them. Institutions announce changes long before they are voted on. Movements deal with changes at every meeting and on every agenda. Change is a big deal to institutions because it is seen as a potential threat to those currently in leadership. Movements see change as a necessary tool in order to achieve their objectives. Refer back to your pretest. How many "stills" and how many "alreadys" did you mark? Institutions tend to respond to change influencers only after a considerable amount of time. Movements tend to embrace changes earlier and view themselves as having already embraced an influence that others are only beginning to consider.

Movements also leave a little "slack in the rope" in order to respond to the drivers that are determined to be opportunistic for the organization. This concept is known as "organizational slack." It is not wise to commit all of the organization's resources at the beginning of the fiscal year. The reason for this is that I can almost guarantee that some opportunity to respond to one of society's trends will occur during the year, an opportunity that has greater potential impact than any of the programs or policies that your organization can foresee advancing at the beginning of the year. Need convincing? Recall Hurricane Katrina.

Balancing Urgency and Hope

Changes occur nearly every day in organizations as new people are added, tasks are accomplished, and hopes realized. But organizations will not transform or change significantly without the passion to do so. In this chapter I have identified three sources of potential passion in organizations. No matter what the source, the passion must either be directed at moving away from the past or moving toward a future. Organizations either push away from or are pulled toward a new reality. Most organizations strictly employ one source or the other. Agile organizations, however, find a way to balance the passion derived from these two sources. The passion to change from what has been is the passion of *urgency*. The passion to move toward a desired future is the passion of *hope*. Currently, the organizational consulting field is filled with experts promoting one style of transformation over the other. In John Kotter's *Leading Change,* he suggests creating a sense of urgency even if none exists.[17] Other change theories, such as "Appreciative Inquiry," suggest ignoring the past and the problems associated with it and focusing only upon the future.

I believe that the best change efforts come about from a balance of the two passions. In order to bring about lasting change, agile organizations balance urgency and hope. Whether the source of passion stems from the contour, the competition, or internally among the collisions of insiders, elements of urgency and elements of hope can always be found to balance one another. Agile organizations present as many reasons to move toward a new collective future as they do to move away from the present circumstances.

PASSION POSTTEST

For the Passion Posttest, list the seven greatest sources of change currently influencing your organization. List only items that you believe present unique and positive opportunities for your organization. Try to list at least one source of change from your environment, one source of change stemming from similar organizations, and at least one source originating from within your organization.

1.

2.

3.

4.

5.

6.

7.

PASSION DISCUSSION QUESTIONS

1. When is the last time that your organization experienced a complete transformation of its identity or vision? How easily was the transformation implemented?
2. How has the median age of your membership changed in the last ten years? As your organization adds new members and staff, are your drawing from all age groups?
3. How many volunteer hours does your organization benefit from on a monthly basis?
4. How is your organization responding to the dramatic increase of immigrants in the U.S.?
5. How else could your organization benefit from existing technological capabilities?
6. Can you name someone in your organization who might help track trends in the contour? Trends among similar organizations? Identify passions within internal collisions?
7. Is your organization experiencing more transparency or more stealthlike practices?
8. Are there any traditions in your organization that are sacred?
9. Where are mavens and ravens in your organization?
10. Ponder the last organizational change adopted. Did its promoters emphasize urgency or hope?

MEASURING PASSION

For the following list of items, please indicate the extent to which you believe that your organization currently demonstrates these behaviors and activities according to the following schema. As you answer the questions, please draw upon your personal knowledge of your organization during the last six months. Please do not be afraid to use all parts of the spectrum in your responses. Total the responses for your "passion" score.

5 = This is true of my organization almost all of the time
4 = This is true of my organization most of the time
3 = This is true of my organization about half the time
2 = This is seldom true of my organization
1 = I cannot recall a time when my organization did this

Our organization...

_____ knows that it cannot continue doing business as usual.
_____ readily accepts change as a window toward something better.
_____ knows that you cannot live in the past.
_____ clearly has its best days ahead of it.
_____ will change when the bottom line tells it to.
_____ will change when there is something worth changing for.
_____ could be facing a desperate situation in the next five years.
_____ is good at instilling hope in its members.
_____ has leaders who often display a sense of urgency regarding the status quo.
_____ can do anything it sets its mind to do.

Total the scores for your organizational passion total _____.

Total the scores for 1, 3, 5, 7, and 9 _____. This represents your organization's sense of urgency to change..

Total the scores for 2, 4, 6, 8, and 10 _____. This represents your organization's sense of hope for a better future.

10

Embracing Change: *Maturity*

Passion——Maturity
(strength)　　(speed)

MATURITY PRETEST

Maturity involves embracing change. For the maturity pretest, please list the major changes that your organization has attempted over the last several years. Begin with your current year and think in reverse, listing each change that you can recall.

Now, take a look at items that you have listed. Check each box below that corresponds to the changes that you have sought to implement in recent years. Check all that apply.

- ❏ Changes in Identity, Brand
- ❏ Structural Changes
- ❏ System Changes
- ❏ Personnel Changes
- ❏ Changes in Vision
- ❏ Changes in Goals
- ❏ Changes in Objectives
- ❏ New Events
- ❏ Maturity

Have you ever met anyone whom you thought would never grow up? One of the stereotypes of someone who never grows up is someone who is carefree, energetic, and happier than the rest of the world. But, I am not sure that stereotype is true. Most of the people whom I know that never grew up are not really happy. They also are not very carefree because they usually worry about how they are going to survive with little means of support. The typical image that I have of someone who "refuses" to grow up is someone who is suffering the consequences for not having embraced the changes that this person needed to embrace at some earlier point in his or her life. People that never grow up are usually people who avoid change even when all the signs around them are telling them that they should change.

On the other hand, the happiest people that I know are people who have grown up and fulfilled their dreams and achieved their ambitions. They are certainly not always wealthy and are often involved in very altruistic professions where they regularly help others. They are fulfilled individuals who are happy because they are making a difference, setting the pace, or discovering something new.

Growing up involves change. It involves accepting new responsibilities and trying out new things even when they appear initially distasteful. Growing up sometimes means embracing that undesirable task first so that one can have even *more* time for the more enjoyable things after that. Growing up means embracing change. The same is true of organizations. Consider some of the organizations that decided never to grow up. They did not see the need for computers. They were comfortable with the same leaders they had always had. They viewed education as something that employees did to get a job, not excel at one. They had heard of research and development, but always believed that was something for those other organizations. They viewed all trends as fads and all fads as bad. I mention these organizations in the past tense because they are no longer with us. History books and archives are full of such organizations that did not make it because they did not want to change. Mature organizations learn how to embrace and welcome change. Agile organizations view change as an ongoing responsibility, never as a new or extra item to consider.

Organizations that refuse to grow up by refusing to change can remain alive for a long time, but begin to operate like zombies, as Sydney Finkelstein suggests:

> They might continue to do business the way they always have. They might even do it extremely well. But when a problem develops and things stop working the way they did before, managers have no way of knowing they are largely cut off from the outside information they need. What makes these zombie businesses so deceptive is that they are usually *happy* zombies.[1]

Organizational Responses to Change

As we discovered in the previous chapter, an organization must possess a desire to change in order to successfully implement change. Just as no one can force an individual to alter his or her behavior, no one can force an organization to change. Once the passion for change is discovered, however, the organization is only one-half of the way there. The organization must then decide how to respond to the driving force and then follow through with that response. Discovering the passion for change will add strength to the organization. Following through with a response to the change will add speed. This will result in a more agile organization.

In this chapter, I describe four possible organizational responses to change. The responses come from a schema graphed below. The two rows in Figure 10.1 represent different degrees of change. In the Olympic Games, some sports such as gymnastics and diving carry a degree of difficulty attached to each attempted move. It is the same with the organisms called organizations. Some organizational moves carry with them a higher degree of difficulty than others. The organizational responses of adoption and adaptation carry a lesser degree of difficulty, while the organizational responses of emulation and transformation carry a much higher degree of difficulty. A higher degree of difficulty translates into increased cost, time, and energy in order to bring about the desired change. Emulation and transformation involve wholesale changes in either the vision or culture of the organization, while adaptation and adoption do not. Changing either the vision or culture of an organization requires that several other components of the organization be altered in order to bring about the desired change in vision or culture. For more on resistance to change, consult Chris Hobgood's *Welcoming Resistance,* as he outlines the type of resistance that can be anticipated from seven levels of change.[2]

High Level of Difficulty	Emulation	Transformation
Low Level of Difficulty	Adoption	Adaptation
	NEW FOUNDATION	OLD FOUNDATION

The two columns in Figure 10.1 represent the past and the future. Adoption and emulation are built upon foundations that are new. Adaptation and transformation are built upon existing foundations. In the first column, leaders motivate members to change by painting an unacceptable portrait of the organization, as it currently exists. The organizational responses of transformation and adaptation, on the other hand, are based upon integration, and assume that some of the current systems and practices will be carried forward. The motivating factor is not so much that something is wrong, but rather the recognition of opportunities that lie on the horizon beckoning the organization toward change. Column one responses have little desire to continue current practices. Column two responses often view the present state of the organization as a good or desirable state; it is merely that future possibilities are even brighter if the organization can embrace new ideals. Column one responses want to discard certain present practices as quickly as possible. Column two approaches may not want to discard anything, only embrace what is new.

Whether a change is based upon a new or old foundation, all changes come with a warning label. Column one changes always run the risk of discarding too much too soon, only to be forced to recreate it again in the future, usually with less care and effectiveness than the original version. Changes in column two run the risk of becoming bogged down in the complicated efforts of integration and synergism and abandoning the change too quickly due to the long implementation cycle.

I describe each of the four responses to change below in greater detail. As I discuss each change, I have also chosen to illustrate each one using a consistent scenario, that of a local congregation desiring to reach out to a more diverse group than it currently is reaching through its worship and programming opportunities.

Adoption

The first form of organizational change is called "adoption." This change involves a lower level of difficulty and disruption within the organization and is based upon adopting a new foundation, not adapting an existing one. Members or leaders of the organization who feel the need to adopt a new practice in order to adequately respond to the pressures for organizational change may simply add it to the existing practices. Obviously, overdoing this can jeopardize the organization by overloading the present staff and budget as too much is added to an already full plate.

Simply adding a new program to an already existing system is one form of organizational change. I once witnessed a team building illustration that effectively demonstrates the potential overload factor. During the exercise, participants form a circle and then begin to pass a ball around the circle. The facilitator asks each person to remember who threw the ball to him or her and to whom that person threw it to next. This is not that difficult with one ball, but becomes chaotic as more balls are introduced into the system. Eventually, too many balls introduced into the system, leads to too much chaos to handle adequately and the balls begin to fly around the room.

When new programs, new services, new staff, or new products are added, something must give and there is a tendency to give too much attention to the new while disregarding the old. This is especially true when a new form of something is added to an already existing form. Let's consider how the adoption approach to change would respond to the scenario mentioned earlier, that of a local congregation seeking to appeal to a more diverse constituency. One specific approach that many congregations have taken when faced with this opportunity is to add a new worship service, one that differs in style from the existing worship service and seeks to appeal to a new group. Adopting a new worship service can allow the congregation to appeal to two very different target groups simultaneously.

The easiest form of adoption is to divert attention away from an existing practice and redirect it toward a new practice. Several years ago, many congregations offered a worship service on Sunday morning and a worship service on Sunday evening. Some church leaders may not have thought about it, but often these two services also appealed to two different audiences. In many congregations, the Sunday evening worship took on a more didactic approach and appealed to the highly committed members. In other congregations, the evening service was much more evangelistic than the morning service. In either case, over the years, the majority of the Sunday evening worship services have dwindled in attendance and no longer accomplish their intended purposes. The resources from programs that fall into this category can sometimes be redirected toward a new program. Indeed, some leaders have seen this as an opportunity to redirect some of the energy, some of the pastor's time, some of the money for utilities, etc., being poured into the Sunday evening service into a new worship service aimed at a totally new audience. Many have offered the new service on Saturday evening and have attempted to appeal to a younger audience. Obviously, such redirection requires work, but the benefit of this approach is that the new program or service begins with at least a minimal set of resources.

The more difficult form of adoption is to add something new without letting go of any existing service. Organizations do this on a regular basis, but seldom stop to calculate the impact of draining more resources from the existing organization without strategizing adequately where the resources will come from. Because the new is usually added because the old was not achieving the desired results, the temptation is to give all of the attention to the new while neglecting the old. Often very little care is given toward continuing the old form and seldom is the old improved while the new form is being added. Thus, the result is that the new often succeeds at the expense of the old rather than in addition to it. This can be true of any addition to the congregation, not just worship services. When new programs, small groups, ministries, mission emphases, and structures are added to a congregation, there is always the temptation to ignore the older versions. Knowing that this is a possibility can certainly help to avoid this outcome.

In adoption, many organizations do not want to raise the difficult question regarding an unproductive or boring program, so they just ignore it, and, usually, the program does go away. But, there is a sense of "it didn't have to be this way." If the congregation wants to truly maintain the old while launching the new, two teams should be formed: one to implement the new service, and one to improve the old, or at least carry it forward with the same level of energy with which the new is launched. One more note about redirecting existing resources toward a new program. Resources of money, goodwill, space, programming slots, etc., can easily be redirected toward a new program. If the primary resource in the old program, however, was volunteer leadership, then redirecting this resource toward a new program is more like adaptation than adoption.

Nothing is ever successfully implemented without a strategy to make it happen. The strategy of adoption involves demonstrating that the existing form is not meeting the expectations desired, or demonstrating how the new program will achieve new results. Whether it is a worship service, a new product, a new service, or a new facility, the leaders create a penchant for the new by demonstrating the lack of results or gap in the existing offerings of the current organization. The danger of this strategy is that the existing membership can see this as a slam on what has meant so much to them in years past. The key is to emphasize that the old method worked at one time, but is no longer working because the environment, the preferences, the people, or the neighborhood has shifted, which no longer allows the current form to have the same impact that it once did.

In implementing an adoption strategy, I have listed several key questions that should be answered prior to commencing the strategy.

1. What is being released in order to free up resources for the new thing?
2. If nothing is being released, where will the new resources come from?
3. What are the principles upon which the new is based? How consistent are those principles with the current organizational values and identity?
4. What is the overall goal of the new addition?
5. What are three objectives that will bring about that goal?
6. Who needs to be involved to build ownership of it?
7. Where in our existing structure could progress be monitored?
8. What could we measure to see if we are heading in the right direction?
9. Are there any limitations for the implementing group to recognize?
10. What obstacles are typical for this type of addition?
11. How will the organization benefit from the addition?
12. What is an example of an early success story that might be foreseen and celebrated if achieved?

Adaptation

Another form of change that still carries a lower level of difficulty, but is based upon an existing base rather than a new base for the program or service, is adaptation. If the organization has a current practice or service that is being received well by the constituents, they may simply seek to make it better rather than adding a new form of it.

We can return to the example of congregational worship services to illustrate this point. Rather than adding a new worship service, many congregations have adapted their existing worship service by increasing the variety or quality of it, often in hopes of appealing to a more diverse group of people. This style has been termed "blended worship" in which the varied interests of the potential attendees are combined into one service.

While the major issue in adoption is how to garner the new resources, the major issue with adaptation is how to fully understand the needs of those who are not currently being reached by the current program or service. One way of attempting this is through "primary planning," a concept that I introduced in an earlier publication.[3] The concept might be applied to this particular situation by ensuring that those with a primary interest in the outcome (the targeted audience) are involved in the design of the blended worship, rather than those with merely a secondary interest, even if it means gathering input into the worship design from those who are not yet a part of the congregation.

The strategy for implementing an adaptation is to first of all celebrate what currently exists and then show how the outcomes could be expanded by reforming it. One of the best examples of this is when Tiger Woods, the number one golfer in the world, announced several years ago that he was going to redesign his golf swing in order to increase the outcomes from it, even though the current outcomes were more than adequate in the perceptions of the golf world. Some adaptation implementation questions to consider are:

Who is primarily being served by the existing program?
What do they like about the program?
Who is not being reached by the existing program?
How can we discover their needs?
How can we alter what exists to meet their needs?
How will the organization benefit from the adaptation?

More Difficult Changes: Introducing Emulation and Transformation

When an organization needs to do more than merely adopt or adapt, it faces a more difficult form of change. Sometimes adoption or adaptation is not enough. Sometimes an organization needs to do more than add a new program or implement a new incentive system; it needs to completely change its identity or vision. The only way that this can be accomplished is by making dramatic changes throughout the organization. Emulations and transformations typically involve wholesale changes in either the identity of the organization, the vision of the organization, or both.

The chart below details implementation strategies for changing either the identity or the vision of an organization. In the chart, I have listed everything that must be altered to bring about a new vision or a new identity for an organization.

Definitions

Vision–a descriptive picture of the end state you are trying to reach

Goals–desired outcomes, foci, etc.

Objectives–an emphasis with a clear budget and strategy

Events–specific one time event such as a training event

Culture–norms, beliefs, values, brand, etc.

Structure–board configuration and size

Systems–personnel or HR systems, reward or incentive systems, fund-raising, etc.

People–CEO and staff, job descriptions, training, recruitment, etc.

CULTURE	VISION
↓	↓
STRUCTURE	GOALS
↓	↓
SYSTEMS	OBJECTIVES
↓	↓
PEOPLE	EVENTS
↓	↓

As you can see from the figure, bringing about a change in the identity or vision of an organization requires several more changes. For an organization to adopt a new identity, it must also adopt a new structure, new systems, and new leaders or training. Let me illustrate. Years ago, the denomination in which I serve announced they were going to view the local church as their "fundamental unit of mission." Several years later, the denomination is still trying to make this a reality. While several key changes have been made, the stated goal will not become a reality until changes are made in the structure, systems, and people to make it so.

The same is true with vision. Imagine trying to adopt a new vision without implementing any new goals, objectives, or events. In order to bring about change in any single item illustrated above, everything in the column underneath that item must also change. Take a look back at your pretest data. As you read either column from the bottom up, you should see no gaps. You can stop at any level, but all boxes must be checked below that level as you rise toward the top. Any gaps represent an attempted change with less than a full implementation strategy. The pretest data may help the reader see why previously attempted changes have either been successful or not.

Changes in identity and vision involve either the emulation of a new organization or the transformation of the existing one. Emulation is based upon the need to change the current identity or vision, imitating a new one. Transformation involves altering the existing components of the existing organization in order to bring about more desirable outcomes. Both are hard work. When working with groups seeking to make major changes, I sometimes ask if anyone in the group ever had orthodontia work. The analogy helps the group realize that the changes that they are about to embark upon will not be painless and will not be quick. It also helps the group think about the readiness factor that is associated with change. There is a time for major change and a time to delay it, depending upon the identified level of passion for the change. But, when organizations are ready, the outcomes will outweigh the costs. Below, I describe in more detail the final two forms of response to change: emulation and transformation.

Emulation

Emulation strategy assumes that the old is not working anymore and fully embraces every aspect of a new type of organization, a new position within the marketplace, or a new way of being. With emulation, very little care is given toward maintaining anything that currently exists in the organization. The foundation for the new is based upon a model not present in the existing organization. Football teams that emulate a new West Coast offense discard their old offense. Service organizations that try to be like their parent federation discard their old image. Congregations that seek to become a megachurch emulate the practices and forms of other megachurches. Emulations surface because the members no longer trust the current systems and structures. They have lost hope in the present and are searching for a new reality.

Even though an organization may seek to emulate another, emulation does not mean duplication. When an individual seeks to emulate someone else, he or she does not seek to become that person, but rather seeks to practice what the other person practices in order to achieve similar results. An emulation is based upon the assumption that what worked in one organization will work in another with some adjustments for context. The faith component in an emulation lies in trusting the behaviors of the new organization. We have all practiced emulations before–when we learned to ride a bike, to hit a ball, to dive into a pool, or to tie our shoes. Most of us can still hear the voice of a parent or grandparent, friend or neighbor encouraging us to hold the bat a certain way, place our feet on the pedals, or to hold our hands in a certain position even if it felt awkward, all the while trusting in our mentor that this action would yield the results that we wanted to achieve. Eventually, after we learned to ride a bike or hit a ball with a bat or play a song on the piano, we developed our own style for doing so. But in the beginning, replication was necessary.

I also need to point out that organizations may emulate an organization of which they are familiar, or they may emulate an image of what an organization should be. The point is that with emulation, there is very little energy to hang on to anything currently present in the organization. Emulations are often more urgent than transformations because they are based upon the assumption that continuing even one more day under the current structure and system is a recipe for disaster.

Emulations are more often driven by internal collisions in the organization or by knowledge of similar organizations. Transformations are more often driven by an awareness of a changing contour and a need to embrace some of the opportunities contained within it. Emulations are often brought about by organizational crises related to finances or personnel. When an organization can no longer make payroll, it is often ready to become something very different no matter what the cost to the existing structures and systems. One more caution: this strategy can work so well that it can be overused. Crises can be created for nearly every change desired. Another concern is that crises do not always lead to positive changes. The change still requires concerted efforts on the part of the members in order to make something new a reality. "Every crisis doesn't lead to nirvana. Sometimes the ship really does sink."[4]

In addressing the previous scenario of a local congregation seeking to appeal to a broader constituency, an emulation approach would call for several changes to be made, rather than focusing only upon one aspect, such as the worship service. A congregation seeking to emulate another might implement three or four best practices or behaviors of the revered organization such as (1) develop a new worship service, (2) adopt a philosophy of regularly adding new small groups, (3) initiate a comprehensive follow-up procedure to contact every guest, (4) add new technology throughout the building to enhance the media capabilities of the church, including the development of a Web site. As we have discussed in previous chapters, developing objectives to coincide with these goals or developing lead indicators to accompany the lag indicators would be the next step. Emulation approaches normally involve embracing several practices of other organizations that are achieving the results desired.

Emulation approaches more often seek to achieve a new vision rather than create a new culture within the organization. With that in mind, I have listed several discussion questions for consideration in an emulation approach.

1. What is the vision for what we hope to become?
2. What organizations are achieving the results that we hope to achieve?
3. What books or other resources have been recommended by these organizations?
4. What are some of the best practices of these organizations?
5. Based upon these best practices, what are three or four major goals that we can set?
6. How can we achieve each goal?
7. What are the benefits and limitations associated with each goal?
8. What is the timetable to launching each new event?
9. What is our budget for the entire emulation approach?

Transformation

Transformation differs from an emulation in that it assumes that the current organization is productive on many levels, but still requires wholesale changes in order to be more effective. A transformation approach seeks to change what exists into something new. While emulation seeks to add many new things to an organization while discarding many old things, transformation seeks to make all things new. This is typically achieved through changes in the culture or identity of the organization. Consider our intent to help a local congregation appeal to a broader constituency. Since I discussed how to embrace a new vision through emulation, I will discuss how to transform the culture of an organization rather than the vision of an organization. In bringing about the transformation necessary to embrace a new identity, let us address each component in column one of the illustration on page 167.

In order to embrace a new identity, an organization must also alter the structures, systems, and people to reflect the new cultural reality. The structure of any organization includes its service delivery structures (worship services, Sunday school classes, ministry teams, generational groups, etc.) as well as its decision-making structures (committees, councils, boards, etc.). We have already discussed that a congregation might seek to transform its worship service, as well as its service delivery structures, in an attempt to appeal to a broader constituency. One of the ways of doing this is to form a feedback team of people who represent the interests of those whom the congregation is trying to reach. The feedback team might meet with the worship leadership team every week for several weeks to offer feedback both on the upcoming worship service as well as the most recent one, helping the worship leadership team transform the existing worship service into something completely new.

Another service delivery system of traditional congregations is the Sunday school structure. In transforming this structure to appeal to a broader constituency, a good place to start is by asking each Sunday school class to identify the last new person that joined their class. Classes that have not added anyone in awhile could be encouraged to learn from those who have, or, if all classes have operated as closed systems, plans for new classes could be made. In transforming the decision-making structure, the congregation may decide to streamline the decision-making process in order to make rapid change possible as new ideas and new opportunities surface. Some congregations have adopted "single board" structures to accomplish this while others have transformed their committees into ministry teams.

The systems of an organization include the financial system, the personnel system, and the volunteer system. The congregation may seek to transform its financial system by simply asking, "How can we redesign our budget to reflect our new culture and new ideals?" The goal in redesigning the leadership system would obviously be to have the targeted groups well represented in the visible leadership, including the professional staff. Congregations may transform their volunteer systems through skills training and recruitment training.

Finally, the people of the congregation themselves can be transformed by highlighting diversity awareness through existing delivery mechanisms such as preaching and teaching, or by offering classes to learn more about the different needs of generational groups and immigrant groups in the community. As you can see, in order to bring about a transformation, every aspect of the organization must be addressed, including the structures, the systems, and the people who comprise the organization.

Some of the key discussion questions in achieving a transformation include:

1. What are the outcomes that we hope to achieve?
2. What ideals need to be embraced?
3. How can we describe our new identity?
4. What components of our existing organization are off-limits?

5. How can we alter our structures to reflect our new ideals?
6. How can we alter our systems to reflect our new ideals?

Additional Suggestions to Enhance Responses to Change

I have listed below some additional considerations that might aid the change processes described above.

Assigning Responsibility to One Person

Because of their degree of difficulty, both emulation and transformation will benefit from having one person oversee the change process, although adoption and adaptation would benefit from this as well. The job description of such a person is to monitor progress on all fronts. In large organizations, such a person might be a staff member, but a volunteer can also fulfill this role. The person should not be the pastor or CEO, but rather should be a trusted member of the organization who has broad appeal to the existing members: "Whether you call the leader of the change the sponsor, the champion, the czar, change manager, or program manager, the best way to assure the implementation of a strategic change is to clearly assign the responsibility to one person."[5]

Organizational Coupling

Often in organizational change, the leaders desire to increase both the stability and the creativity of the organization at the same time. Traditionally, they sacrifice one or the other, unaware that these dichotomous outcomes are achievable in the same organization by applying different techniques to differing parts of the organization.

The theory of organizational coupling[6] suggests that it is possible to achieve differing types of outcomes in different parts of the organization by altering the "degree of coupling" among component parts. The degree of coupling refers to the levels of interaction among components. Tight organizational coupling leads to outcomes characterized by consistency, stability, accountability, control, and ownership of ideas. Loose coupling, on the other hand, leads to outcomes characterized by variability, innovation, creativity, empowerment, and localized determination.

Maturity within Movements and Institutions

The difference between movements and institutions with respect to change is that movements change with an entrepreneurial style, while institutions change with a focusing style. Institutions tend to emphasize the pain of change. Movements tend to emphasize the benefits of change. Institutions tend to change by emphasizing upon the change processes themselves. Movements tend to change by emphasizing the outcomes that will be achieved if the changes are made.

Agile organizations, on the other hand, do both. Agile organizations are both focused and entrepreneurial.

> The *best* companies are simultaneously focused *and* entrepreneurial. They share the core competency of knowing what to preserve and what to change. Focused on their core strategy and true to their core values, they are dynamic implementers of the strategy. These companies are innovative on both the strategic and execution levels, that is, adding new activities and improving the execution of existing activities. The desire to be the best in their chosen business runs deep and compels internal change.[7]

Agile organizations also anticipate change rather than react to it. At the Australian Institute of Sport, Damian Farrow teaches athletes how to develop the intuitive side of their response to change. Farrow "spends a lot of time simply trying to determine what it is experts see that amateurs don't. Among other things, he uses an eye-motion tracker to record where virtuoso players are looking during clutch situations, such as when passing while under pressure from multiple defenders coming from multiple directions."[8] Farrow teaches athletes how to rely more on their intuition than their physical response in order to help athletes become more agile. Agile organizations also rely more on intuition than do stagnant organizations. They seek to respond to opportunities quickly. They make changes in structure that will allow the organization to respond more quickly to other prospects down the road. They encourage their members to try things, to experiment, to occasionally chase rabbits, and to enter the forest where no one else has entered. Agile organizations become learning organizations.[9]

Maturity and Balance

Balance is extremely important in change. One of the balances that must be achieved in the change process is balancing the past with the future. In the same way that leaders balance the past and the future in bringing to the surface the passion of the organization, they must again balance the past and the future in bringing about the changes necessary to help the organization mature into the kind of organization it is capable of becoming. Leaders must decide what to *maintain* from the past as well as what to *create* in the future. Both are necessary for an organization to mature. Many organizations suffocate from a deluge of programs, products, or services because they add every year and never abandon anything. Likewise, many organizations cocoon from a timidity about venturing into a new arena of products or services even though all other sources of input are calling upon the leaders to do so. Agile organizations constantly ask, "What needs to be created in this organization in order for it to mature?" Organizational leaders who also consistently ask, "What must be abandoned in order for this creation to occur?" will receive much more energetic responses to their first question. Creativity and abandonment must be balanced in order for either to occur. Agile leaders achieve a balance of the past (coincident patterns) and the future (temporal patterns) within their organizations.

A second balance that must be achieved to bring about successful change is in the balancing of principles and practices. As I alluded to earlier, bringing about a new vision through emulation implies adopting new practices, and trusting that they will yield new, more desirable results. Bringing about a new identity is more focused upon principles than practices, as each existing component of the organization is transformed to reflect the new ideals and principles embraced by the members. But, whether working on identity or vision, agile organizations emphasize both practices and principles. Practices without principles will lead to mismanagement. Principles without practices will yield no results. Agile organizations balance principles with actual practices to bring about the desired change.

Strengthening an organization requires change. Growth, development, and improvement all imply that changes will take place. Agile organizations recognize that change processes underlie every activity in the organization. Change is necessary in order to produce new outcomes. Agile organizations never reorganize, restructure, retool, or reengineer, because they are constantly making adjustments in order to produce better outcomes.

MATURITY POSTTEST

For the maturity posttest, refer to your pretest at the beginning of this chapter. If you have ever sought to embrace a wholesale organizational change in either culture or vision, and discovered that you had gaps in your implementation, seek to address those gaps below. Check each area below not addressed in the pretest and indicate some initial steps that you might take to mature this neglected area within your organization.

❏ Changes in Identity, Brand
❏ Structural Changes
❏ System Changes
❏ Personnel Changes
❏ Changes in Vision
❏ Changes in Goals
❏ Changes in Objectives
❏ New Events

MATURITY DISCUSSION QUESTIONS

The discussion questions for this chapter have been embedded within the chapter in each of the four responses to change: namely, adoption, adaptation, emulation, and transformation.

MEASURING MATURITY

For the following list of items, please indicate the extent to which you believe that your organization currently demonstrates these behaviors and activities according to the following schema. As you answer the questions, please draw upon your personal knowledge of your organization during the last six months. Please do not be afraid to use all parts of the spectrum in your responses. Total the responses for your "passion" score.

5 = This is true of my organization almost all of the time
4 = This is true of my organization most of the time
3 = This is true of my organization about half the time
2 = This is seldom true of my organization
1 = I cannot recall a time when my organization did this

Our organization...

_____ is keenly aware of what it does well.
_____ would never be called obsolete.
_____ recognizes the strengths that exist in our current systems.
_____ is not afraid to abandon the old if needed.
_____ would rather alter what we have than embrace something new.
_____ creates what it needs in order to respond to a new opportunity.
_____ can reinvent itself when needed.
_____ is not afraid to let go of an old program.
_____ often adapts what we do based upon the "best practices" of others.
_____ understands that something must go when a new thing is added.

Total the scores for your organizational maturity total _____.

Total the scores for 1, 3, 5, 7, and 9 _____. This represents your organization's ability to maintain or modify existing elements to contribute to an overall change strategy.

Total the scores for 2, 4, 6, 8, and 10 _____. This represents your organization's ability to abandon and create a new world.

Epilogue

A CLOSING POSTTEST

For the final posttest, I invite you to reflect upon the organizational outcomes that have been described in this book by ranking the outcomes according to their relative strength in your organization. If you saved your pretest, compare your posttest answers with your pretest answers. What did you learn about the organizational outcomes? Did your rankings change as a result of your learnings?

Step One: Give each person in your team (or you can do this exercise individually) ten 3x5 cards. Look at the list of organizational outcomes on page 13. As one person reads each outcome, place the name of the outcome on one of your 3x5 cards. As each subsequent outcome is read and described as in the earlier portion of the introduction, begin to place the cards in a rank order according the relative strength of each outcome within your organization. For instance, after you have written "identity" and "vision" on your first two cards, place the one that is currently stronger within your organization at the top and the other below it. Continue in this manner until you have placed all of your ten outcomes in descending order according to the relative strength of each outcome as it currently exists in your organization.

Step Two: Share your rankings with one other person.

Step Three: Seek to come to consensus with this person so that you end up with one rank order list between the two of you.

Step Four: Place the names of the ten outcomes on a sheet of newsprint and record each pair of rankings on the newsprint in order to build the perspective of the entire group.

Step Five: Take a look at the results. Where do the majority of people in your team or organization believe the relative strengths are of each of the ten outcomes?

Step Six (optional): Seek to come to consensus as a group on the relative strengths of each outcome.

Notes

Introduction

[1]Michael Lombardo and Robert Eichinger, *The Leadership Machine: Architecture to Develop Leaders for Any Future* (Minneapolis: Lominger, 2000), 5.

[2]Marcus Buckingham, *Now, Discover Your Strengths* (New York: The Free Press, 2001), 6.

[3]Jeffrey Hawkins, *On Intelligence* (New York: Times Books, Henry Holt and Company, 2004).

[4]Ibid., 60.

[5]Ibid., 57.

[6]Ibid., 59.

Chapter 1–Embracing Culture: *Identity*

[1]Aubrey Malphurs, *Advance Strategic Planning: A New Model for Church and Ministry Leaders* (Grand Rapids: Baker Books, 2005), 42–44.

[2]Luthar K. Snow, *The Power of Asset Mapping* (Herndon, Va.: The Alban Institute, 2004).

[3]Steven Sample, *The Contrarian's Guide to Leadership* (San Francisco: Jossey-Bass, 2002), 145–47.

[4]Tracey Wong Briggs, "We the second-graders at Providence Elementary," *USA Today*, April 17, 2007, 9D.

[5]Richard Southern and Robert Norton, *Cracking Your Congregation's Code* (San Francisco: Jossey-Bass, 2001), 24.

[6]David Roozen and James R. Nieman, eds., *Church, Identity, and Change* (Grand Rapids: Eerdmans, 2005), 604.

[7]Kenneth T. Walsh, "A Sinking Presidency," *US News & World Report*, 142, no. 17 (May 14, 2007): 43.

[8]James Ludema, *The Appreciative Inquiry Summit: A Practitioner's Guide for Leading Large-Group Change* (San Francisco: Berrett-Koehler, 2003).

[9]Mark Lau Branson, *Memories, Hopes, and Conversations: Appreciative Inquiry and Congregational Change* (Bethesda, Md.: The Alban Institute, 2004).

[10]Leonard Berry, *Discovering the Soul of Service* (New York: The Free Press, 1999), 200.

[11]Carol Pearson, *Awakening the Heroes Within: Twelve Archetypes to Help Us Find Ourselves and Transform Our World* (San Francisco: Harper, 1991).

[12]Carol Pearson, *Organizational and Team Culture Manual* (Gainesville, Fla.: Center for Applications of Psychological Type, 2004), 14.

[13]Available at: http://www.capt.org, The Center for Applications of Psychological Type.

[14]Thomas J. Neff and James M. Citrin, *You're in Charge, Now What?* (New York: Crown Business, 2005), 64.

[15]Ronald Heifetz and Marty Linsky, *Leadership on the Line* (Boston: Harvard Business School Press, 2002), 65.

Chapter 2–Embracing Culture: *Vision*

[1]Peter Koestenbaum, *Leadership: The Inner Side of Greatness* (San Francisco: Jossey-Bass, 1991), 105.

179

[2]Ronald Heifetz and Marty Linsky, *Leadership on the Line* (Boston: Harvard Business School Press, 2002), 102.

[3]Ibid., 102–7.

[4]Melinda Davis, *The New Culture of Desire: Five Radical Strategies that Will Change Your Business and Your Life* (New York: The Free Press, 2002), 15.

[5]Ibid., 29.

Chapter 3–Embracing Purpose: *Mission*

[1]More information available at: http://en.wikipedia.org/wiki/The_Mission_ (film).

[2]More information available at: http://www.missioncollege.org.

[3]Quoted in Malcolm Gladwell, *Blink: The Power of Thinking without Thinking* (New York: Little, Brown and Company, 2005), 119–20.

[4]Sodality is a concept, usually employed in Catholic circles, that describes a task-oriented group or ministry. They are sometimes called "confraternities." In the same context, modality describes a local church or a judicatory, such as a diocese. For more information see http://en.wikipedia.org/wiki/Sodality.

[5]Rob Yule, "Burning, Not Yet Consumed, Paradoxes of the Church," sermon available at http://www.stalbans.org.nz/teachings/rob_yule/the_church/church1. htm.

[6]Herbert Simon, "On the Concept of Organizational Goal," *Administrative Science Quarterly* 9, no. 1 (June 1964): 1–22.

[7]Darrell L. Guder and Lois Barrett, *Missional Church: A Vision for the Sending of the Church in North America* (Grand Rapids: Eerdmans, 1998), 80.

[8]Jim Collins, *Good to Great* (New York: Harper Collins, 2001), 203.

[9]John Carver, *Boards that Make a Difference* (San Francisco: Jossey-Bass, 1997), 59.

[10]Michael Porter, *Competitive Strategy: Techniques for Analyzing Industries and Competitors* (New York: Free Press, 1980).

[11]B. D. Henderson, *Henderson on Corporate Strategy* (Campbrige: Abt Books, 1979), 164–66.

[12]Porter, *Competitive Strategy,* 16.

Chapter 4–Embracing Purpose: *Results*

[1]John Carver, *Boards that Make a Difference* (San Francisco: Jossey-Bass, 1997), 50.

[2]Paul Niven, *Balanced Scorecard: Step-by-Step for Government and Non-Profit Agencies* (New Jersey: John Wiley & Sons, 2003), 15.

[3]Ibid., 32.

[4]Robert S. Kaplan and David P. Norton, *The Balanced Scorecard: Translating Strategy into Action* (Cambridge, Mass.: The President and Fellows of Harvard College, 1996).

[5]Phillip Schlechty, *Shaking Up the Schoolhouse: How to Support and Sustain Educational Innovation* (San Francisco: Jossey-Bass, 2002), 72.

[6]Rod Napier and Rich McDaniel, *Measuring What Matters* (Mountain View, Calif.: Davies-Black, 2006), 84.

[7]Kathleen A. Cahalan, *Projects That Matter: Successful Planning and Evaluation for Religious Organizations* (Bethesda, Md.: Alban Institute, 2003), 1.

[8]Ibid.

[9]John Marchica, *The Accountable Organization* (Palo Alto, Calif.: Davies-Black, 2006), 64.

[10]Leonard Berry, *Discovering the Soul of Service* (New York: The Free Press, 1999), 74.

[11]Michael Hammer and James Champy, *Reengineering the Corporation, A Manifesto for Business Revolution* (San Francisco: Harper & Row, 2001), 128.

[12]Thomas Bandy, *Moving off the Map: A Field Guide to Changing the Congregation* (Nashville: Abingdon Press, 1988), 23.

[13]Patrick Lencioni, *Silos, Politics and Turf Wars* (San Francisco: Jossey-Bass, 2006), 178.

[14]John G. Miller, *QBQ! The Question Behind the Question, Practicing Personal Accountability at Work and in Life* (New York: G.P. Putnam's Sons, 2001).

[15]James Ludema, *The Appreciative Inquiry Summit: A Practitioner's Guide for Leading Large-Group Change* (San Francisco: Berrett-Koehler, 2003), 183.

[16]Ibid., 184.

[17]James Collins, *The Power of Catalytic Mechanisms* (Boston: Harvard Business Review, 1999), 72.

[18]James Collins and Jerry Porras, *Built to Last: Successful Habits of Visionary Companies* (New York: Harper Collins, 1994), 156.

[19]Patrick J. McKenna and David H. Maister, *First Among Equals* (New York: The Free Press, 2002), 169.

[20]John Carver, *Boards that Make a Difference* (San Francisco: Jossey-Bass, 1997), 50.

[21]Laurie Fendrich, "A Pedagogical Straitjacket," *Chronicle of Higher Education*, June 8, 2007, B6–B8. Available at: http://chronicle.com/weekly/v53/i40/40b00601. htm.

Chapter 5–Embracing People: *Potential*

[1]Howard Gardner, *Multiple Intelligences* (San Francisco: Basic Books/Harper Collins, 1993).

[2]Available at: http://www.Lominger.com, Lominger International: A Korn/Ferry Company.

[3]Steven J. Stein and Howard E. Book, *The EQ Edge: Emotional Intelligence and Your Success* (Toronto: Multi-Health Systems, 2000), 24.

[4]Reuven Bar-On, *Bar-On Emotional Quotient Inventory* (Toronto: Multi-Health Systems, 1997).

[5]Carol Pearson, *Awakening the Heroes Within: Twelve Archetypes to Help Us Find Ourselves and Transform Our World* (San Francisco: Harper, 1991), 7.

[6]Information available at: http://www.capt.org/catalog/Archetype-Assessment-Personal.htm.

[7]Marcus Buckingham and Donald O. Clifton, *Now, Discover Your Strengths* (New York: The Free Press. 2001), 6.

[8]Leonard Berry, *Discovering the Soul of Service* (New York: The Free Press, 1999), 159.

Chapter 6–Embracing People: *Performance*

[1]Edward L. Deci and Richard M. Ryan, "The What and Why of Goal Pursuits: Human Needs and Self-Determination of Behavior," *Psychological Inquiry* 11 (2000): 227–68.

[2]Available at: http://www.Lominger.com, Lominger International: A Korn/Ferry Company.

[3]Rod Napier and Rich McDaniel, *Measuring What Matters* (Mountain View, Calif.: Davies-Black, 2006), 146.

[4]Nancy Shute, "The 18–Second Doctor," *US News & World Report*, 142, no. 11 (March 26, 2007): 14.

[5]Alex C. Pasquariello, "Grant Makers," *Fast Company* (April 2007): 32.

[6]Napier and McDaniel, *Measuring*, 146.

[7]Paul Stoltz, *Adversity Quotient @ Work* (San Francisco: William Morrow, 2000), 213.

[8]Gregory Huszczo, *Tools for Team Leadership* (Mountain View, Calif.: Davies-Black, 2004), 63.

[9]Susan Wheelan, *Creating Effective Teams* (Thousand Oaks, Calif.: Sage Publications, 1999).

[10]George Cladis, *Leading the Team-Based Church: How Pastors and Church Staffs Can Grow Together into a Powerful Fellowship of Leaders* (San Francisco: Jossey-Bass, 1999), 106.

[11]Jordan Lewis, *Trusted Partners: How Companies Build Mutual Trust and Win Together* (New York: The Free Press, 1999), 20.

[12]Michael Marquardt, *Action Learning: Solving Problems and Building Leaders in Real Time* (Mountain View, Calif.: Davies-Black, 2004), 95.

[13]Ibid., 37.

[14]Patrick McKenna and David H. Maister, *First Among Equals* (New York: The Free Press, 2002), 171–72.

[15]Lewis, *Trusted Partners,* 109.

Chapter 7–Embracing Assets: *Capacity*

[1]Jim Collins, *Good to Great* (San Francisco: Harper Collins, 2001).

[2]George Barna, *How to Increase Giving in Your Church* (Ventura, Calif.: Regal Books, 1997), 50.

[3]Michael Cortes, "Three Strategic Questions about Latino Philanthropy," *New Directions for Philanthropic Fundraising,* no. 8, ed. Charles H. Hamilton and Warren F. Ilchman (San Francisco: Jossey-Bass, 1995), 28.

[4]Stella Shao, "Asian American Giving: Issues and Challenges," *New Directions for Philanthropic Fundraising,* 56.

[5]James Hudnut-Buemler, *Generous Saints: Congregations Rethinking Ethics and Money* (Bethesda, Md.: The Alban Institute, 1999), 53.

[6]Ibid., 54.

[7]Barna, *How to Increase Giving,* 130.

[8]Jean Fairfax, "Black Philanthropy: Its Heritage and Its Future," *New Directions for Philanthropic Fundraising,* 12.

[9]Barna, *How to Increase Giving,* 92.

Chapter 8–Embracing Assets: *Allocations*

[1]Douglas John Hall, *The Steward* (New York: Friendship Press, 1990), 40.

[2]Ibid., 41.

[3]Ibid., 45.

[4]Ron Valet, *Stepping Stones of the Steward* (Grand Rapids: Eerdmans, 1989), 50.

[5]Peter Block, *Stewardship: Choosing Service over Self-Interest* (San Francisco: Berrett Koehler, 1993), 44.

[6]David Beebe, "Stewards and Witnesses," *Journal of Stewardship,* vol. 50 (1998): 31.

[7]Jean Fairfax, "Black Philanthropy: Its Heritage and Its Future," *New Directions for Philanthropic Fundraising,* no. 8, ed. Charles H. Hamilton and Warren F. Ilchman (San Francisco: Jossey-Bass, 1995), 14.

[8]Information available at: http://www.pulpitandpew.duke.edu.

[9]Hall, *The Steward,* 45.

[10]Loyde Hartley, *Understanding Church Finances: The Economics of the Local Church* (New York: Pilgrim Press, 1984).

[11]Ibid.

Chapter 9–Embracing Change: *Passion*

[1]Ken Matejka and Al Murphy, *Making Change Happen on Time, on Target, on Budget* (Mountain View, Calif.: Davies-Black, 2005), 20.

[2]Ian Ayres, as quoted in Jerry Adler, "Era of the Super Cruncher," *Newsweek* (September 3, 2007): 42.

[3]Ibid., 42.

[4]Matejka and Murphy, *Making Change Happen*, 25.

[5]Haya El Nasser, "Where Will Everybody Live?" *USA Today*, October 27, 2006, 1A.

[6]The statistics below come from Silla Brush, "A Nation in Full," *U.S. News & World Report* (October 2, 2006): 54.

[7]The statistics for this paragraph also come from ibid., 53.

[8]Stephen Johnson, *Emergence* (New York: Scribner, 2001), 40–41.

[9]Scott Adams, quoted in Malcolm Gladwell, "Fast Talk: What's the Biggest Change Facing Business in the Next 10 Years?" *Fast Company* (March 2006): 22.

[10]Jack Carroll, *God's Potters: Pastoral Leadership and the Shaping of Congregations* (Grand Rapids: William Eerdmans, 2006).

[11]Tim Brown, quoted in Gladwell, "Fast Talk," 22.

[12]John Mackey, quoted in ibid., 23.

[13]Cited in Mark Penn, "Little Trends, Big Impacts," *US News & World Report* (September 10, 2007): 33.

[14]Ibid., 33.

[15]Malcolm Gladwell, *The Tipping Point: How Little Things Can Make a Big Difference* (Boston: Little, Brown and Company, 2000), 67.

[16]Liz Nickles, *The Change Agents* (New York: St. Martin's Press, 2001), 64.

[17]John Kotter, *Leading Change* (Boston: Harvard Business School Press, 1996).

Chapter 10–Embracing Change: *Maturity*

[1]Sydney Finkelstein, *Why Smart Executives Fail and What You Can Learn from Their Mistakes* (London: Portfolio, A Penguin Book, 2003), 167.

[2]Chris Hobgood, *Welcoming Resistance* (Bethesda, Md.: The Alban Institute, 2001).

[3]C. Jeff Woods, *Congregational Megatrends* (Bethesda, Md.: Alban Institute, 1996), 135–48.

[4]Patrick Lencioni, *Silos, Politics and Turf Wars* (San Francisco: Jossey-Bass, 2006), 124.

[5]Ken Matejka and Al Murphy, *Making Change Happen on Time, on Target, on Budget* (Mountain View, Calif.: Davies-Black, 2005), 115.

[6]Further information on this topic available at: http://en.wikipedia.org/wiki/Loose_coupling.

[7]Leonard Berry, *Discovering the Soul of Service* (New York: The Free Press, 1999), 74.

[8]Jennifer Kahn, "Mind Games," *Wired* (June 2007): 129.

[9]Peter M. Senge, *The Fifth Discipline: The Art & Practice of the Learning Organization* (New York: Doubleday, 1990).